Fuenteovejuna

A Dual-Language Book

Lope de Vega

Edited and Translated by
STANLEY APPELBAUM

DOVER PUBLICATIONS, INC.
Mineola, New York

Bibliographical Note

This Dover edition, first published in 2002, includes the original Spanish text of *Fuenteovejuna,* reprinted from a standard Spanish edition, together with a new English translation by Stanley Appelbaum, who also wrote the Introduction and footnotes. (See the Introduction for further bibliographical details.)

Theatrical Rights

This Dover edition may be used in its entirety, in adaptation, or in any other way for theatrical productions, professional and amateur, in the United States, without permission, fee, or acknowledgment. (This may not apply outside of the United States, as copyright conditions may vary.)

Library of Congress Cataloging-in-Publication Data

Vega, Lope de, 1562–1635.
    [Fuente Ovejuna. English & Spanish]
    Fuenteovejuna : a dual-language book / Lope de Vega / edited and translated by Stanley Appelbaum.
       p. cm.
  ISBN-13: 978-0-486-42092-9 (pbk.)
  ISBN-10: 0-486-42092-2 (pbk.)
   I. Appelbaum, Stanley. II. Title.

PQ6459 .F7513 2002
862'.3—dc21

2002017524

Contents

INTRODUCTION

Spanish Theater in the Time of Lope de Vega

Lope de Vega (1562–1635) is the most prolific and representative author of the "Golden Age" Spanish theater, and many call him the greatest, as well.[1] Every history of world drama dwells admiringly on this Siglo de Oro (for some literary genres, the Golden Age is considered as lasting from about 1550 to 1700; for the drama, it is substantially equivalent to the first three quarters of the seventeenth century), but the drama of the period was not unchanging and monolithic, and it permitted of numerous specific variations. Here it can be discussed in very general terms only.

Golden Age drama did not issue from a vacuum. Spanish-language (that is, Castilian, as opposed to Catalan, etc.) play texts of the medieval period are incredibly sparse in comparison with those in other western European countries, but from about 1500 on, under strong influence from precocious Italy, important Renaissance playwrights appeared in Spain. The pastoral plays of Juan del Encina (?1468–?1530); the chivalric and religious plays, farces, and masques of Gil Vicente (?1460–?1539, a Portuguese who wrote both in his own language and in Castilian); and the five-act, single-verse-form plays of Bartolomé de Torres Naharro (?1485–?1520) were all written for private performances in royal or noble circles.

By mid-sixteenth century, public theaters were active, featuring works by men like Lope de Rueda (?1509–1565), who specialized in one-act prose comedies (pasos). As the century progressed, scholarly university plays were put on, and Italian comedy troupes toured Spain. The generation before Lope was dominated by Miguel de Cervantes (1547–1616), author of Don Quixote, who wrote both verse tragedies and prose one-acters (entremeses), and by Juan de la Cueva (?1550–1610), whose four-act tragedies are credited with introducing

---

1. Others award the palm to Calderón (Pedro Calderón de la Barca, 1600–1681), whose plays are generally better constructed, more polished, and more profound.

national themes, drawn from ballads and chronicles, into the Spanish theater.

Lope's day saw the full flowering of these trends, and he himself consolidated and consecrated (though he did not invent them) several features of the *comedia nueva,* or *comedia española,* the chief dramatic form of the period.[2] The following paragraphs summarize the leading characteristics of the *comedia* (= "play") in the time of Lope's maturity (roughly 1610 to 1635).

The playwright (*poeta*) sold the play outright to the actor-manager (*autor*) of an acting company, who most often staged it in a *corral* (a purpose-built theater in an innyard or in a space left vacant between existing buildings). Originally the *corrales* were owned and run by religious fraternities, which used the admission money to finance their own hospitals. Later, the *corrales* were leased to companies of actors (Lope stated that, in his lifetime, the number of companies in Madrid had increased from 2 to 40); later still, the *corrales* (in Madrid, at least) were taken over by the municipality.

A typical *corral*[3] was a long rectangle, with the stage at the far end opposite the entrance. The two long sides had galleries for seating, while the groundlings stood in the "pit." The stage had lateral entrances, a simple backcloth, one or two upper levels,[4] and, on the main level, a "discovery space," a small area closed off by doors or curtains which could be opened at opportune moments for significant revelations. There was no formal scenery, and just a bare minimum of props, though costuming was important.

A new play might be given only two, three, or four performances, so that new plays were in constant demand; hence, the astronomical numbers of plays written in the period; and hence, the undue haste that could affect the work of such popular purveyors as Lope. Performances began in the late afternoon and were over by dark. Before, after, and between the acts of a full-length play (*comedia*), the audience was regaled with curtain-raisers, skits, and music.

The subject matter of the *comedia* was very varied. There were historical plays, plays based on Bible stories and saints' lives, comedies of

---

2. The second major kind of play was the *auto sacramental,* a long one-act verse religious allegorical morality or mystery play, performed on holy days on elaborate floats. Lope wrote some good examples, but Calderón perfected the *auto.*   3. Restored examples still exist in Alcalá de Henares and in Almagro (where the opening scene of *Fuenteovejuna* takes place).   4. In *Fuenteovejuna,* an upper level represents the battlements from which Ferdinand and Isabella's banners fly in the scene depicting the recapture of Ciudad Real by their forces.

amorous intrigue abetted by scheming servants, family tragedies, etc. There were fashionable topics at certain times, such as the rash of plays about lower-class people defending their honor against overbearing noblemen. (Royalty was normally not presented as overbearing; rather, it seemed as if kings could do no wrong, and a king serves as an abrupt *deus ex machina* at the end of many a play.) There were very few outright tragedies; in general, even the most serious plays had comic moments, and the final outcome is usually optimistic, with good conquering evil, so that the term "tragicomedy" would apply to those *comedias* that are not strictly comedies in our sense.

Lope's practice assured the victory of the three-act form for the *comedia* in the seventeenth century, the three acts usually containing the exposition, complication of the plot, and denouement, respectively. The pseudo-Aristotelian, neoclassical unities of time and place[5] were usually not observed. As in the Elizabethan public theaters, scene changes were fluid and were made known chiefly by means of the dialogue; printed stage directions are very sparse and fail to supply locations.

Roles were usually standardized. Acting companies had players who specialized in young lovers', old men's, heavies', and kings' parts, etc. Female roles were played by actresses from 1608 on. A particularly characteristic role type in this period was the *gracioso* ("comic"), often a shrewd and witty but selfish, greedy, and cowardly servant or other lower-class figure. The *gracioso* might merely inject punning one-liners, but in the better plays he could be crucial to the action.

One aspect of *comedias* that translations cloak, or severely disguise, is that they are in verse, and, in fact (chiefly thanks to Lope), in a variety of verse forms (usually involving rhyme or assonance) corresponding to the content of the dialogue (see the analysis of verse forms in *Fuenteovejuna* later in the Introduction). Very frequently, popular song forms were sprinkled in to amuse the groundlings.

With some exceptions, scenes of violent action are heard from offstage, and not enacted in the audience's view.

There is frequently a final tag at the very end of the play, in which the audience is addressed directly and in which the title of the play is mentioned.

The texts of *comedias* that we possess do not necessarily represent in every detail what the playwrights originally wrote. They were often printed hastily for immediate profit, and were sometimes based on

---

5. Theorists had determined that the action of a proper play should occur within a 24-hour period, and that the scene should be as unvaried as possible, even a single room.

the recollections of actors who played roles in the plays in question. Attributions to playwrights (who rarely oversaw the publication) were often erroneous, a successful author like Lope being credited for work not his in order to deceive the public.

Other major Spanish playwrights of the 1610–1635 period are: Castro (Guillén de Castro y Bellvís, 1569–1631, from Valencia), author of the pair of plays *Las mocedades del Cid* (Youthful Exploits of El Cid), the first of which was the direct basis of Pierre Corneille's *Le Cid*; the Mexican-born Alarcón (Juan Ruiz de Alarcón y Mendoza, ?1580–1639), author of *La verdad sospechosa* (Truth You Can't Trust), the direct basis of Corneille's *Le menteur*; and "Tirso de Molina" (Gabriel Téllez, ?1580–1648), who may or may not have written the play that is the earliest known work about Don Juan, *El burlador de Sevilla* (The Seducer from Seville).

After about 1620 there was a tendency to furnish more scenery in the *corrales*, and the importance of royal and noble private theaters in palaces increased. The private theaters featured elaborate, sumptuous staging and more learned plays, often based on Greco-Roman mythology, in which music was an important constituent (there were actual operas). Lope wrote some plays for these private theaters in his later years, and Calderón's career would have been quite different without such venues.

The Career of Lope de Vega

Many biographical details about Lope, especially about his poorly documented childhood and youth, have been taken by authors of reference works from his own publicistic statements and those of his hero-worshipping contemporaries. There are many uncertainties, inconsistencies, and outright contradictions.

He definitely was born in Madrid in 1562. His father, also a passionate man, had followed a woman there from his hometown in northern Spain; overtaken and reclaimed by his wife, he had settled in Madrid, working as an embroiderer, a simple artisan. Lope Félix de Vega Carpio, as the future author eventually styled himself, was said to have been a child prodigy with early literary gifts. Certainly he enjoyed a decent schooling, at least partly thanks to favors from well-placed people who recognized his potential. It is said that in 1572 he attended a grammar school run by the poet and musician Vicente Espinel (1550–1624), author of the major picaresque novel of 1618

Vida del escudero Marcos de Obregón (Life of the Squire M. de O.). In 1574 Lope entered a secondary school run by Jesuits, where he may have begun writing plays. The patronage of the bishop of Ávila opened the doors of the prestigious university of Alcalá de Henares to him in 1577, and some believe that he also attended the University of Salamanca in 1582.

Moving on to less disputed terrain: In 1583 he joined a Spanish expedition to the Azores, a pocket of resistance to Spain's annexation of Portugal, which had begun in 1580; it was probably in the same year that, back home, he began a liaison with Elena Osorio, whose father and complacent husband were actors. In December of 1587 Lope was accused of defaming her family in lampoons after discovering that he was being ousted from her affections by another man. In 1588 he was exiled from Castile for two years, from Madrid for eight. Nevertheless, he managed to abduct a (willing) noblewoman, Isabel de Urbina, whom he married by proxy, but with whom he lived only a couple of weeks before he joined the Invincible Spanish Armada.

Returning safely from that disastrous expedition, he went to live in Valencia, where (take your pick!) he either imbibed the best of his stagecraft from the flourishing local "school" of playwrights, or else established that "school" by his own example. In 1590, living in Toledo after the two years' exile from Castile was over, he began his subcareer (which lasted his entire life) of serving noblemen (as secretary, adviser, pimp, etc.). By 1592 he was in the service of the then Duke of Alba, residing in Alba de Tormes, near Salamanca, until 1595, when his wife died and he was able to return to Madrid a year early, thanks to relentment on the part of Elena's father.

As early as the following year, he was back on trial for illicit relations with the noblewoman Antonia Trillo. In 1598 he entered into what many considered a loveless marriage for money with Juana de Guardo, a wealthy butcher's daughter; in that same year he may have first met his next serious mistress, the actress Micaela de Luján. In the following years he shuttled between his legitimate family in Toledo and his illegitimate one in Seville, both of which were growing.

By 1599 at least, Lope was almost exclusively a playwright; he has been called the first popular dramatist of modern times to earn most of his money from plays (this was thanks to the huge quantity of them, rather than to any great earnings from a single play). In 1604 the first collective volume of his plays was published; eventually there would be 25 volumes, but he personally supervised only volumes 9 through 20 (1617–1625); later ones were supervised by a son-in-law; the last three were posthumous, Volume 25 appearing as late as 1647; these volumes do not represent his entire output.

In 1609 he joined the first of several religious fraternities he eventually would belong to. His nature contained a strong religious side that was genuine, flaring up especially in times of crisis, but never completely overcoming his amatory urges. In 1610, after periods of Madrid residence alternating with periods in Toledo, Seville, and Valladolid, he established a permanent home in Madrid on the street now called Calle de Cervantes, where a reconstructed "Casa de Lope" house-museum is a popular tourist attraction.

In 1612 Lope's legitimate son Carlos Félix died at the age of six, and the boy's mother, his second wife, died in 1613. Now Lope's religious leanings led him to seek holy orders, and he was ordained in 1614. But other affairs followed, and in 1616 he entered a lasting relationship with Marta de Nevares, whom of course he could not marry. A severe illness led to her blindness in 1623; she went mad in 1628, but Lope stood by her until her death in 1632.

Further personal tragedies darkened the end of Lope's days. In 1634, the year in which his last play was performed, his beloved son (by Micaela) Lope Félix was drowned near Venezuela on a pearl-fishing expedition. In 1635 one of his daughters eloped with a cynical nobleman; Lope died later that year.

Though he was constantly under fire from neoclassicist critics for his laissez-faire dramaturgy, and from such scholarly writers as the outstanding poet Luis de Góngora (1561–1627) for the "incorrectness" of his style and the populisms he affected, Lope was astoundingly successful in his own lifetime. He was dubbed "the phoenix of intellects," and Cervantes called him a *monstruo de la naturaleza* ("phenomenon"). It was the highest praise to say of anything whatsoever (not merely literary productions) that it was "by Lope."

The number of plays he wrote was once reckoned as 1,500, or even 1,800. Of the 501 extant plays that have been attributed to him, the best authorities (figures differ!) consider 314 to be absolutely genuine, 27 probably by him, and 73 possibly by him. The types of plays he wrote (some classifications are as finicky as Polonius's categories of plays in *Hamlet*) include: middle-class amorous intrigues (plays of *capa y espada*, "cape and sword"), chivalric plays, plays based on the Bible and saints' lives, plays based on Spanish and foreign history, plays about peasant honor, and courtly mythological plays. His sources were chronicles, ballads, popular proverbs and sayings, previous plays, and Italian stories and novels. Whatever the subject or source, he set every-thing in a milieu that was recognizable to his audience as being typically Spanish and up-to-date in tone.

Some critics have divided his dramatical career into three phases, characterized by increasingly firm control of his means; but there are great plays from all periods, and speed of composition was always one of his strong (and weak) points: he once boasted that more than a hun-dred of his plays had been written in a day each. There is no doubt of his enormous facility in writing; freshness, sincerity, and spontaneity do much, to outweigh occasional carelessness or routine. (Not that he was remiss or devil-may-care: his manuscripts attest to extensive cor-rection and rewriting.)

Out of his staggering output, a mere handful of his plays are reprinted over and over again, and called his best. Besides *Fuenteove-juna*, these include: *Peribáñez y el comendador de Ocaña* (Peribáñez and the Commander of Ocaña; written between 1609 and 1612, first published 1614), *El perro del hortelano* (The Dog in the Manger; written between 1613 and 1615, first published 1618), *El caballero de Olmedo* (The Knight of Olmedo; written between 1615 and 1626, first published 1641), *El mejor alcalde, el rey* (The King the Best Magistrate; written between 1620 and 1623, first published 1635), and *El castigo sin venganza* (Punishment without Revenge; first per-formed 1631, first published 1635).

In addition to plays, Lope wrote a vast quantity of works in other genres (just about everything current in his day except picaresque novels), his lyrics being especially highly regarded. These lyrics, both sacred and profane, include hundreds of sonnets, as well as ballads, epistles, eclogues, odes, songs, and didactic poems. He also wrote long epic poems, a mock epic, and an important poem about his prac-tice as a playwright, the "Arte nuevo de hacer comedias en este tiempo" (New Art of Writing Plays in This Day and Age; 1609). His longer prose works include the pastoral novel *La Arcadia* (1598) and the novel in dialogue *La Dorotea* (1632), about his youthful romance with Elena Osorio.

Some plays by Lope have long been in the international repertoire (though English translations are not plentiful and are sometimes dis-figuring), yet it has been claimed that he was not truly a world-class dramatist, being too insular, as well as superficial (especially in com-parison with his exact contemporary, Shakespeare). Obviously, how-ever, very few people are acquainted with his entire oeuvre, and the time has not yet come for a definitive evaluation.

Lope's Play *Fuenteovejuna*

Composition and Publication. *Fuenteovejuna* (the title also occurs as two words) is generally considered one of Lope's best plays, and it is probably the most famous one internationally. It was written between 1611 and 1618, and many literary historians narrow this down to between 1612 and 1614.[6] It was first published in the twelfth volume of collected plays by Lope: *Dozena parte de las comedias de Lope de Vega Carpio,* Madrid, 1619, printed for the widow of Alonso Martín by the bookseller Alonso Pérez.[7]

Sources. "Fuenteovejuna did it" was still a current saying in Lope's time. His direct source for his exposition of the political situation, the sieges of Ciudad Real, and the peasant uprising was Francisco de Rades y Andrada's *Crónica de los tres órdenes y caballerías de Santiago, Calatrava y Alcántara* (Chronicle of the Three Knightly Orders S., C., and A.; 1572). Moreover, the Fuenteovejuna uprising is mentioned in two works by the lexicographer Sebastián de Covarrubias that were published shortly before Lope wrote the play: the *Emblemas morales* of 1610 and the *Tesoro de la lengua castellana o española* of 1611.

Historical Background. Fuenteovejuna (today officially called Fuente Obejuna) is in the province of Córdoba in Andalusia; Córdoba was recaptured from the Moors in 1236. The town has long been known for its production of honey, and the true etymology of its name is from *abeja,* so that it originally meant Bee Spring.[8] The town was given to the Knights of Calatrava in 1460 by Castilian king Enrique (Henry) IV; at that time, the Grand Master of that military order of knights-friars (which had been founded in 1158 to help fight the Moors) was Pedro Téllez Girón, father of the young Master in the play. The royal donation was annulled in 1465, but in 1468 Fernán

---

6. The wider range of years is quite reliable, being based on dated listings by Lope (the play is not included in a 1611 list; it is included in a 1618 list). The narrower range of years, hypothetical but believable, is based on an ingenious study of the rhyme and stanza schemes preferred by Lope at different periods of his career.   7. There were two editions with identical title-page wording but different heraldic designs; one of these editions is known in a number of printings. There are slight textual differences in each case. Another play on the same subject was written later by the Sevillan author Monroy (Cristóbal de Monroy y Silva, 1612–1649).   8. The English title *Sheep's Well* for the play is also unfortunate because what we normally associate with "well" is a dug well, which is *pozo* in Spanish. *Fuente* (as a synonym of *manantial*) means a natural wellspring or natural fountain.

Gómez, the Chief Commander[9] of Calatrava, took it back by force; thus, historically, there had been great political tension even before the peasant uprising, which occurred on the night between April 22 and 23, 1476.

When Enrique IV died in 1474, the uncertainty about the succession to the throne led to civil war and to war with Portugal. One faction favored Enrique's sister Isabel (Isabella), who had married Prince Fernando (Ferdinand) of Aragon (later King Fernando V of Aragon). The other faction favored Enrique's daughter Juana, who had married Alfonso V of Portugal. Juana's enemies dubbed her "Juana la Beltraneja," claiming that her natural father was not Enrique, but the courtier Beltrán de la Cueva. Alfonso warred against Fernando and Isabel, the "Catholic monarchs," but was defeated in 1479. After quelling unruly noblemen (including the military orders) at home, Fernando and Isabel, who had united all of Christian Spain except Navarre, attacked the last Moorish stronghold on the peninsula, the kingdom of Granada, which capitulated in 1492. (They are also famous for financing Columbus, instituting the Inquisition, and expelling the Jews from Spain.)

Rodrigo Téllez Girón (1458–1482), son of Pedro, had become Grand Master at the age of 8 when his father abdicated; Pope Paul II insisted that his paternal uncle, Juan Pacheco, "assist" him officially (Juan had already died by the year when the play takes place, when Rodrigo was 18). Juan's son, Diego López Pacheco (like his father before him, Marquess of Villena), was the guardian of Juana la Beltraneja. (The Count of Urueña was a brother of Rodrigo's.)

Some Features of the Play. *Fuenteovejuna* is one of Lope's plays that are based on Spanish history. It also falls within the category of "evil Commander versus honorable peasant" plays that were a distinctive trend in the Spanish theater between about 1605 and 1620; the glorification of peasant life has been seen as a measure to woo people back to the land at a time when the attractions of city dwelling were injuriously depopulating the countryside.

Fuenteovejuna, which is some 20% shorter than the average Lope play, has been called badly organized, and the Ciudad Real and Catholic Monarch scenes have sometimes been cut from stage productions on the grounds of being a disruptive secondary plot. Careful

---

9. *Comendador Mayor.* "Commander" is the normal English equivalent of *comendador,* but it is etymologically incorrect. A *comendador* is an official who has been given an *encomienda,* a grant of populated territory that supplies his income. In the Order of Calatrava, the Chief Commander was second only to the Grand Master.

reading shows that this is not so: the Commander personally links the town events to the broader national events (his comings and goings to battle and back to town are crucial to the detailed progress of the play), and the townspeople participate in the national events by transferring their allegiance to the Catholic Monarchs.

It is true that certain passages (such as the list of fashionable euphemisms for physical and moral defects, and the diatribe against astrologers) are expendable or detachable showpieces (other "arias," such as Laurencia's praise of home cooking and rural comforts, are more obviously related to the play's main themes);[10] but some of the uneventful interludes are crucial to the plot. For instance, the debate on the meaning of love (during which we first meet Frondoso, Barrildo, and Mengo) dwells on the play's underlying message of love, social harmony, and unselfishness (the townspeople eventually overcome all ills by sticking together through thick and thin); in addition, this debate, in which Mengo appears to be selfish and unloving, creates suspense later on when his testimony at the torture trial is so essential to everyone's well-being.[11]

The Characters. The townspeople either speak in a conventional rural fashion, using wrong words, dialect forms, and archaisms; or else declaim in impossibly learned terms. The Commander (by far the most dynamic character), Master, monarchs, and courtiers generally use elevated, poetically heightened speech.

Frondoso is like the hero of a pastoral romance, much more noble than an ordinary peasant, though he knows his station in society. Laurencia, in her earthy resistance to the Commander's gentle or rough seduction, is like the typical *serranilla* ("mountain girl") of numerous medieval and Renaissance poems. The romance between Frondoso and Laurencia represents the almost obligatory love interest in Spanish historical plays.

Mengo is the *gracioso* of this play, but a very special one. In typical *gracioso* fashion, he is not intrinsically highminded, he mangles words, he is gluttonous, and he has no hesitation in informing the Catholic Monarchs about the state of his buttocks. But, on the other hand, he bravely defends Jacinta and he doesn't let his neighbors down at their most critical moment.

---

10. It has been said that Golden Age Spanish playwrights included various excursuses in order to educate the general public, who had no opportunity for formal learning.   11. Another indication that Lope was not as careless, slipshod, and uninterested in this play as some critics have asserted is the careful sprinkling of animal imagery: the Commander is constantly comparing the townspeople to lowly domestic or timid animals, whereas they keep referring to him and his servants as beasts of prey.

The "interchangeability" of the minor characters (the other towns-people, the Commander's servants), the lack of special characterization in their sayings and doings, has been seen as a plus in this play in which the collective nature of the town's actions is emphasized.[12]

The Poetry. The poetic form of Spanish Golden Age plays is one of their chief components, not to be neglected. The following rhyme and stanza schemes are used in *Fuenteovejuna:*

The most prevalent form (one might call it the normal dialogue form) is *redondillas* (8-syllable[13] quatrains rhyming ABBA).

The second most frequent scheme in the play is the *romance,* based on the scheme of medieval narrative ballads, and traditionally used for "messenger's speeches" in plays. The *romance* consists of an indefinite even number of 8-syllable lines, every second one of which assonates on the same pair of vowels. Thus, for instance, in the first *romance* passage in the play, the Commander's report to the Master about the political situation, every other line ends in a word with the vowels A and O (*AltO, clArO, maestrAzgO,* etc.). Other *romance* passages are: Flores's report on the taking of Ciudad Real by the Master, the report of the councilmen from Ciudad Real, the entire last scene of Act One, Cimbranos's report of the danger to Ciudad Real, the ballad song performed at the wedding (this *romance* has a special refrain in different meter), the entire end of Act Two beginning with the Commander's interruption of the wedding, the scene in which Laurencia appears disheveled and rouses both the men and the women to revolt, and Flores's report on the uprising.

The *romancillo* is the 6-syllable scheme used in the song welcoming the Commander in Act One.

Tercetos (11-syllable terza rima) is used in the passage where the town gives gifts to the Commander, and in the opening scene of Act Three down to Laurencia's entrance.

Octavas (11-syllable ottava-rima stanzas) occur in the opening scene of Act Two down to the Commander's entrance, and during the actual violent uprising of the peasants.

Endecasílabos blancos (pentametric blank verse) are used in the scene of the Master's defeat at Ciudad Real.

---

12. There is no local color in the play, no Andalusian customs or speech patterns, no reference to the town's famous honey. But there is an amusing historical reference to the novelty of printing at the time the events took place.   13. In Spanish 8-syllable verse, there are 8 syllables when the line ends in a feminine rhyme or assonance, but actually only 7 when the rhyme is masculine, and 9 when the rhyme word is trisyllabic and stressed on the first syllable. (The same variation applies to lines of other syllable counts.)

The *villancico* form is used for the shorter songs at the wedding and at the celebration immediately after the uprising (they are mainly 8-syllable stanzas rhyming ABBAACC).

One *soneto* (sonnet) occurs in Act Three; it is spoken by Laurencia as she anxiously awaits the coming of Frondoso (just before the torture scene).

In this edition, the beginnings of stanzas and of *romance* passages are indented. Occasionally a line of verse necessary to complete a rhyme scheme, or a few syllables necessary to complete a line, may be missing, with no injury to the meaning of the text as it stands. These instances may have been slips by Lope or by the printer of the first edition. It has been said that Lope was revolutionary in this play by assigning to peasant characters some rhyme schemes (such as *tercetos*) that were traditionally the preserve of characters from the nobility.

Evaluation of the Play. *Fuenteovejuna* does not seem to have made any special impression in its own day. During the nineteenth century, it was increasingly translated and performed, and by the end of that century, it was being praised loudly by eminent literary historians who perceived it as an unusual revolutionary statement. In the twentieth century, it was called "the first proletarian drama" and it was often staged as a political gesture.[14] But, in actuality, the townspeople of Fuenteovejuna in the play are merely changing masters, placing themselves in the hands of the monarchs in the belief (shared by Lope) that this move will be advantageous for them. They are so far from being intrinsically rebellious that they are really searching for a more suitable (less crude) master to kowtow to (in Freudian terms, they need a "father figure").

Even though the play has thus sometimes decked itself in false colors (through no fault of Lope's), and though it is still being attacked for the various shortcomings it offers to view (sometimes only to a cursory, superficial view), it continues to be held in wide esteem, and to serve in numerous anthologies (sometimes, unfortunately, in translations that falsify its nature) as an example of the best in Spanish theater.

The Nature of This Edition

If not an absolute novelty, the translation offered here is at least a rarity in several significant ways. For one thing, it is absolutely complete,

---

14. There was even a Bolshoi ballet, *Laurencia,* based on it (1939).

not more or less condensed and/or paraphrased to skirt difficulties[15] or to avoid giving offense (e.g., by omitting anti-Semitic remarks). For another thing, it is not "freely adapted," but strives to be as accurate and as close to the original as possible. To achieve these goals, the translation is not in absolute prose (which masks the original intent) nor in any of the previously published English verse forms that depart in line count, and in other, more serious ways, from the Spanish. Instead, without attempting to mimic the original meter and rhymes or assonances—a practice inevitably destructive of accuracy—it conveys the meaning line for line, except in some instances where the difference in syntax between the two languages necessitates redistribution of the textual content within the extent of two (very, very rarely, more than two) lines. The handling of Spanish proper nouns is intentionally not perfectly consistent: people's names are usually kept in their Spanish form, while place names are usually given in their normal English forms.

In the Spanish text, reprinted from a good edition, the spelling is modernized, except when that would alter a given word form, rhyme, etc., injudiciously. (This limited modernization is the practice of most modern Spanish editors.) Punctuation is regularized.

In both the Spanish and the English text of this edition, the original 1619 edition is generally followed with regard to stage directions and scene changes, unlike some modern Spanish editions and translations, which add (sometimes infelicitously) very specific scene locations (e.g., "A hall in the house of the Master of Calatrava" for the opening scene). It seemed preferable to emulate the fluidity of Lope's stage, and to let the reader gather the locations (which sometimes are not very specific) from the dialogue, the way Lope's audience did. It will be noted that the stage directions are sometimes defective, failing to indicate the entrance or exit of some characters, or to identify them fully. In the most confusing cases, this edition adds a few words in square brackets in the translation, or supplies an explanatory footnote.

The list of characters in this edition attempts to list all of them (not

---

15. One of the myths most widely spread by Lope scholars is that of the crystalline clarity of his style (it may have been much clearer to his original audience). If he is so clear, why are there at least a dozen conflicts in *Fuenteovejuna* alone in footnote interpretations in Spanish-language editions? (The most significant alternative explanations of difficult passages are presented in the footnotes to this new translation.) Rare and archaic vocabulary, old inflectional forms, fuzzy syntax, and probable misprints all add to the modern reader's problems. Idioms and wordplays are sometimes hard to identify, as is proved by some particularly mangled English translations.

always the case in some editions), and in the order of their first ap-
pearance; it also supplies the abbreviations used to indicate the
speakers in the main text in order to save space. The designation of
the characters (who may be referred to in different ways at different
times in the original Spanish text) has been regularized in this edition,
although the translator is still not sure how many different
Fuenteovejuna councilmen actually appear! (Is the one at the opening of Act Three possibly a third councilman, different from both Juan
Rojo and Cuadrado? It makes no difference at all in production.)

Fuenteovejuna

PERSONAS

El comendador (Fernán Gómez) [COM.]
Flores [FLO.]
Ortuño [ORT.]
El maestre de Calatrava (Rodrigo Téllez Girón) [MAE.]
Pascuala [PAS.]
Laurencia [LAU.]
Frondoso [FRO.]
Barrildo [BAR.]
Mengo [MEN.]
Músicos [MUS.]
Alonso [ALO.]
Esteban [EST.]
Juan Rojo [JUAN]
Reina doña Isabel [ISA.]
Rey don Fernando [REY]
Don Manrique [MAN.]
Dos regidores de Ciudad Real [REG. 1.º, REG. 2.º]
Un regidor [REG.]
Leonelo [LEO.]
Un labrador [LAB.]
Cimbranos [CIM.]
Jacinta [JAC.]
Un soldado [SOL.]
Un juez [JUEZ]
Un niño [NIÑO]
[Ciudadanos, séquito de los reyes, etcétera]

CHARACTERS

The Commander (Fernán Gómez) [COM.]
Flores [FLO.] } servants of the Commander
Ortuño [ORT.]
The Master of Calatrava (Rodrigo Téllez Girón) [MAS.]
Pascuala [PAS.]
Laurencia [LAU.]
Frondoso [FRO.] } peasants, inhabitants of Fuenteovejuna
Barrildo [BAR.]
Mengo [MEN.]
Musicians [MUS.]
Alonso [ALO.] } joint mayors of Fuenteovejuna
Esteban [EST.] (Esteban is Laurencia's father)
Juan Rojo [JUAN] councilman of Fuenteovejuna, Laurencia's uncle
Queen Isabella [ISA.]
King Ferdinand [KING]
Don Manrique [MAN.] a courtier
Two City Councilmen of Ciudad Real [COU. 1, COU. 2]
A Town Councilman (of Fuenteovejuna) [COU.] (named Cuadrado)
Leonelo [LEO.] a lawyer
A Peasant (inhabitant of Fuenteovejuna) [PEA.]
Cimbranos [CIM.] a soldier in the employ of the Commander
Jacinta [JAC.] a peasant, inhabitant of Fuenteovejuna
A Soldier (in the service of the Master) [SOL.]
A Judge [JUD.]
A Young Boy (inhabitant of Fuenteovejuna) [BOY]
[Townspeople, royal retinue, etc.]

The play takes place in the year 1476 in Fuenteovejuna and other localities in southern and central Spain.

Acto primero

Salen el COMENDADOR, FLORES *y* ORTUÑO, *criados.*

COM.:   ¿Sabe el maestre que estoy
           en la villa?
FLO.:   Ya lo sabe.
ORT.:   Está, con la edad, más grave.
COM.:   ¿Y sabe también que soy
           Fernán Gómez de Guzmán?
FLO.:   Es muchacho, no te asombre.
COM.:   Cuando no sepa mi nombre,
           ¿no le sobra el que me dan
           de comendador mayor?
ORT.:   No falta quien le aconseje
           que de ser cortés se aleje.
COM.:   Conquistará poco amor.
              Es llave la cortesía
           para abrir la voluntad,
           y para la enemistad
           la necia descortesía.
ORT.:   Si supiese un descortés
           cómo lo aborrecen todos,
           y querrían de mil modos
           poner la boca a sus pies,
              antes que serlo ninguno,
           se dejaría morir.

Act One

Enter the COMMANDER, *with his servants* FLORES *and* ORTUÑO.

COM.:   Does the Master know that I am
in the city?[1]

FLO.:   By now he knows.

ORT.:   He's becoming more mature as he gets older.

COM.:   And does he also know that I am
Fernán Gómez de Guzmán?

FLO.:   ? He's just a boy, don't let it surprise you.

COM.:   Even if he doesn't know my name,
isn't he more than satisfied with my title
of Chief Commander?

ORT.:   There's no lack of people who advise him
to refrain from being courteous.

COM.:   He'll win little love that way.
Courtesy is the key
to gaining good will,
just as foolish discourtesy
is the key to enmity.

ORT.:   If a discourteous man knew
how everyone loathes him
and would like in a thousand ways
to defame his character viciously,[2]
rather than behave that way
he'd see himself die.

1. Almagro, the residence of the Grand Master of Calatrava. This city is located roughly halfway between Madrid and Seville, about fifteen miles from Ciudad Real.
2. This is a tentative rendering of an obscure idiomatic expression not elucidated in dictionaries, annotated editions of the play, or previous translations.

5

FLO.:   ¡Qué cansado es de sufrir!
    ¡Qué áspero y qué importuno!
      Llaman la descortesía
    necedad en los iguales,
    porque es entre desiguales
    linaje de tiranía.
      Aquí no te toca nada:
    que un muchacho aún no ha llegado
    a saber qué es ser amado.

COM.:   La obligación de la espada
      que le ciñó el mismo día
    que la cruz de Calatrava
    le cubrió el pecho, bastaba
    para aprender cortesía.

FLO.:   Si te han puesto mal con él,
    presto le conocerás.

ORT.:   Vuélvete, si en duda estás.

COM.:   Quiero ver lo que hay en él.

Sale el MAESTRE DE CALATRAVA, *y acompañamiento.*

MAE.:   Perdonad, por vida mía,
    Fernán Gómez de Guzmán,
    que agora nueva me dan
    que en la villa estáis.

COM.:   Tenía
    muy justa queja de vos;
    que el amor y la crianza
    me daban más confianza,
    por ser, cual somos los dos,
      vos, maestre en Calatrava,
    yo, vuestro comendador
    y muy vuestro servidor.

MAE.:   Seguro, Fernando, estaba
      de vuestra buena venida.
    Quiero volveros a dar
    los brazos.

COM.:   Debéisme honrar,

FLO.:   How tiresome it is to put up with!
          How unpleasant and annoying!
               Discourtesy is called
          foolishness when the parties are of equal rank,
          because between those of different ranks
          it is a kind of tyranny.
               In this case, it is no insult to you,
          because a boy has not yet come
          to know what it means to be loved.

COM.:   The obligation imposed by the sword
               he girded on on the same day
          that the Cross of Calatrava
          covered his breast, should have been enough
          to teach him courtesy.

FLO.:   If people have alienated him from you,
          you'll soon learn when you meet him.

ORT.:   Go back home if you're in doubt.

COM.:   I want to see what there is in him.

          Enter the MASTER OF CALATRAVA, *with his retinue.*

MAS.:   Upon my life, forgive me,
          Fernán Gómez de Guzmán,
          because only now have I been informed
          that you were in the city.

COM.:   I had
          a very just complaint about you;
          because I had more confidence
          in your love and upbringing,
          we two being what we are,
               you the Master of Calatrava,
          and I your chief commander
          and your humble servant.

MAS.:   Fernando,[3] I was unaware
               of your welcome arrival.
          I wish to offer you
          my open arms again.

COM.:   You ought to honor me,

---

3. The full form of the Christian name is used when not immediately followed by
the family name; this is a grammatical trait of older Spanish.

que he puesto por vos la vida
entre diferencias tantas,
hasta suplir vuestra edad
el pontífice.

MAE.:   Es verdad.
Y por las señales santas
  que a los dos cruzan el pecho,
que os lo pago en estimaros,
y, como a mi padre, honraros.

COM.:   De vos estoy satisfecho.

MAE.:   ¿Qué hay de guerra por allá?

COM.:   Estad atento, y sabréis
la obligación que tenéis.

MAE.:   Decid, que ya lo estoy, ya.

COM.:   Gran maestre don Rodrigo
Téllez Girón, que a tan alto
lugar os trajo el valor
de aquel vuestro padre claro,
que, de ocho años, en vos
renunció su maestrazgo,
que después por más seguro
juraron y confirmaron
reyes y comendadores,
dando el pontífice santo
Pío segundo sus bulas,
y después las suyas Paulo,
para que don Juan Pacheco,
gran maestre de Santiago,
fuese vuestro coadjutor;
ya que es muerto, y que os han dado
el gobierno sólo a vos,
aunque de tan pocos años,
advertid que es honra vuestra
seguir en aqueste caso
la parte de vuestros deudos,
porque muerto Enrique cuarto,
quieren que al rey don Alonso
de Portugal, que ha heredado,

because I have risked my life for you
   in the midst of all these conflicts,
even to the point of persuading the Pope to waive
the minimum-age rule for your appointment.

MAS.:   That's true.
And I swear by the sacred symbol
   of the Cross on your breast and mine
that I repay you for it by esteeming you
and honoring you like a father.

COM.:   I am contented with you.

MAS.:   How is the war going in those parts?

COM.:   Be attentive, and you will learn
what obligations you have.

MAS.:   Speak, because now I *am* attentive.

COM.:   Grand Master Don Rodrigo
Téllez Girón,[4] you who have been borne
to this exalted station by the valor
of that famous father of yours
who, when you were eight, renounced
the position of Master in your favor,
a position that was later made more secure
by the oaths and confirmations
of kings and commanders,
the Holy Father Pius II
granting his papal bulls,
and Paul II his own afterwards,
provided that Don Juan Pacheco,
Grand Master of Santiago,
would be your assistant:
now that he is dead, and you have been given
the reins of government personally,
despite your youth,
understand that your honor demands
that in this situation you adhere to
your kinsmen's party;
because, Enrique IV having died,
they want King Alfonso
of Portugal, who has inherited

---

4. See the Introduction for the historical background to this long speech, and for the Master's career and family connections.

por su mujer, a Castilla,
obedezcan sus vasallos;
que aunque pretende lo mismo,
por Isabel, don Fernando,
gran príncipe de Aragón,
no con derecho tan claro
a vuestros deudos, que, en fin,
no presumen que hay engaño
en la sucesión de Juana,
a quien vuestro primo hermano
tiene agora en su poder.
Y así, vengo a aconsejaros
que juntéis los caballeros
de Calatrava en Almagro,
y a Ciudad Real toméis,
que divide como paso
a Andalucía y Castilla,
para mirarlos a entrambos.
Poca gente es menester,
porque tiene por soldados
solamente sus vecinos
y algunos pocos hidalgos,
que defienden a Isabel
y llaman rey a Fernando.
Será bien que deis asombro,
Rodrigo, aunque niño, a cuantos
dicen que es grande esa cruz
para vuestros hombros flacos.
Mirad los condes de Urueña,
de quien venís, que mostrando
os están desde la fama
los laureles que ganaron;
los marqueses de Villena,
y otros capitanes, tantos,
que las alas de la fama
apenas pueden llevarlos.
Sacad esa blanca espada,
que habéis de hacer, peleando,
tan roja como la cruz;

Castile through his wife,
to be obeyed by his vassals;
although the same claim is made,
through Isabel, by Don Fernando,[5]
the great prince of Aragon,
but not with so clear a right
in the eyes of your kinsmen, who, in short,
find no deception
in the succession of Juana,
whom your cousin
now has in his power.
And so, I have come to advise you
to assemble the Knights
of Calatrava at Almagro
and capture Ciudad Real,
which is like a mountain pass
between Andalusia and Castile,
facing both kingdoms.
Not many combatants are needed,
because the city's soldiers consist
merely of its own inhabitants
and a few lesser noblemen
who defend Isabel
and call Fernando king.
It will be a good thing, Rodrigo, though
you are a mere boy, to strike awe in all those
who say that that Cross is too big
for your weak shoulders.
Reflect on the counts of Urueña,
from whom you are descended; they are
showing you, secure in their fame,
the laurels they once won;
and on the marquesses of Villena
and other great captains so numerous
that the wings of fame
can scarcely carry them.
Draw your "white," untried sword,
which, in battle, you must make
as red as your Cross;

5. Ferdinand and Isabella, the future patrons of Columbus.

porque no podré llamaros
maestre de la cruz roja
que tenéis al pecho, en tanto
que tenéis la blanca espada;
que una al pecho y otra al lado,
entrambas han de ser rojas;
y vos, Girón soberano,
capa del templo inmortal
de vuestros claros pasados.

MAE.:   Fernán Gómez, estad cierto
que en esta parcialidad,
porque veo que es verdad,
con mis deudos me concierto.

Y si importa, como paso
a Ciudad Real, mi intento,
veréis que como violento
rayo sus muros abraso.

No porque es muerto mi tío,
piensen de mis pocos años
los propios y los extraños
que murió con él mi brío.

Sacaré la blanca espada,
para que quede su luz
de la color de la cruz,
de roja sangre bañada.

Vos, ¿adonde residís
tenéis algunos soldados?

COM.:   Pocos, pero mis criados;
que si de ellos os servís,
pelearán como leones.
Ya veis que en Fuenteovejuna
hay gente humilde, y alguna
no enseñada en escuadrones,
sino en campos y labranzas.

MAE.:   ¿Allí residís?

because I won't be able to call you
Master of the red Cross
that you wear on your breast as long as
your sword is still white;
because, one of them on your breast and the other at your side,
they must both be red;
and you, excellent Girón,
must be the protective cloak[6] of the immortal temple
of your illustrious ancestors.

MAS.:   Fernán Gómez, rest assured
that, in this party strife,
since I see where the truth lies,
I am on the side of my kinsmen.
    And, if my participation is necessary
as a means to capture Ciudad Real,[7]
you will see me like a violent
lightning flash burning its walls.
    Just because my uncle is dead,
let no kinsman or stranger,
in view of my youth, think
that my vigor and spirit died with him.
    I shall draw my white sword,
so that its gleam will be
the same color as my Cross,
once it is bathed in red blood.
    And you, in your residence
do you have any soldiers?

COM.:   Not many, but they're my personal servants,
so that, if you make use of them,
    they will fight like lions.
For, you see, in Fuenteovejuna
the people are of low rank, and some of them[8]
not trained for the battlefield,
    but for pastures and grain fields.

MAS.:   Your residence is there?

---

6. The Spanish has an untranslatable wordplay on the Master's family name of Girón (a homonym of *jirón*, "scrap of cloth") and "cloak." 7. Or (punctuating: *si importa, como paso, a Ciudad Real mi intento*): "If, as I believe, my attempt captures Ciudad Real." 8. Or (punctuating: *humilde y alguna,*): "of low rank and few in numbers."

COM.:   Allí
de mi encomienda escogí
casa, entre aquestas mudanzas.
MAE.:   Vuestra gente se registre.
COM.:   Que no quedará vasallo.
MAE.:   Hoy me veréis a caballo
poner la lanza en el ristre.

Vanse, y salen PASCUALA *y* LAURENCIA.

LAU.:   Mas ¡que nunca acá volviera!
PAS.:   Pues a la he que pensé
que cuando te lo conté,
más pesadumbre te diera.
LAU.:   ¡Plega al cielo que jamás
le vea en Fuenteovejuna!
PAS.:   Yo, Laurencia, he visto alguna
tan brava, y pienso que más,
y tenía el corazón
brando como una manteca.
LAU.:   Pues ¿hay encina tan seca
como esta mi condición?
PAS.:   ¡Anda ya! Que nadie diga:
de esta agua no beberé.
LAU.:   ¡Voto al sol que lo diré,
aunque el mundo me desdiga!
¿A qué efeto fuera bueno
querer a Fernando yo?
¿Casárame con él?
PAS.:   No.
LAU.:   Luego la infamia condeno.
¡Cuántas mozas en la villa,
del comendador fiadas,
andan ya descalabradas!
PAS.:   Tendré yo por maravilla
que te escapes de su mano.
LAU.:   Pues en vano es lo que ves,
porque ha que me sigue un mes,
y todo, Pascuala, en vano.

COM.:	There, of all places in my domain, I elected to live, during these political ups-and-downs.
MAS.:	Let your people be enrolled.
COM.:	None of my vassals will remain behind.
MAS.:	Today you shall see me on horseback placing my lance at the ready.

The above exit. Enter PASCUALA *and* LAURENCIA.

LAU.:	I wish he had never returned here!
PAS.:	Well, by my faith, I thought that, when I told you about it, I'd be giving you greater distress.
LAU.:	May it please heaven that I never see him in Fuenteovejuna!
PAS.:	As for me, Laurencia, I've seen girls who resisted love as much as you do, if not more so, but whose hearts were as soft as butter.
LAU.:	But is there an oak tree as dried up as my nature is?
PAS.:	Come, now! No one should ever say: "I won't drink that water."[9]
LAU.:	I swear that I *will* say it, even if the whole world contradicts me! What would be the good of my loving Fernán Gómez? Could I ever marry him?
PAS.:	No.
LAU.:	Well, then, I condemn the dishonor. Look at all the girls in town who trusted the Commander's words and have now been hurt!
PAS.:	I'll consider it a miracle if you escape his clutches.
LAU.:	Well, then, what you see is an illusion, because he's been pursuing me for a month, and all in vain, Pascuala.

A womanizer

---

9. That is, "That will never happen to me!"

Aquel Flores, su alcahuete,
y Ortuño, aquel socarrón,
me mostraron un jubón,
una sarta y un copete;
   dijéronme tantas cosas
de Fernando, su señor,
que me pusieron temor;
mas no serán poderosas
   para contrastar mi pecho.

PAS.:   ¿Dónde te hablaron?

LAU.:   Allá
en el arroyo, y habrá
seis días.

PAS.:   Y yo sospecho
que te han de engañar, Laurencia.

LAU.:   ¿A mí?

PAS.:   Que no, sino al cura.

LAU.:   Soy, aunque polla, muy dura
yo para su reverencia.
   Pardiez, más precio poner,
Pascuala, de madrugada,
un pedazo de lunada
al huego para comer,
   con tanto zalacatón
de una rosca que yo amaso,
y hurtar a mi madre un vaso
del pegado canjilón;
   y más precio al mediodía
ver la vaca entre las coles,
haciendo mil caracoles
con espumosa armonía;
   y concertar, si el camino
me ha llegado a causar pena,
casar una berenjena
con otro tanto tocino;
   y después un pasatarde,
mientras la cena se aliña,
de una cuerda de mi viña,
que Dios de pedrisco guarde;

> That Flores, his pimp,
> and Ortuño, that sly fox,
> have offered me a bodice,
> a necklace, and a headdress;
>   they told me so much
> about their master Fernando
> that they frightened me;
> but all the things they said won't have the power
>   to overcome my feelings.

PAS.: Where did they speak to you?

LAU.:   There
> by the stream, about
> six days ago.

PAS.:   And I suspect
>   that they'll fool you yet, Laurencia.

LAU.: Me?

PAS.:   No—the parish priest!

LAU.: Though I'm still young, I'm very severe
> with regard to His Reverence.[10]
>   Goodness, Pascuala!
> I much prefer a piece
> of ham in the morning
> placed on the fire for breakfast,
>   with a huge hunk
> of a bread roll that I've kneaded,
> and a glass of wine filched from my mother
> out of the caulked jug;
>   and at noon I much prefer
> to watch the cow amid the cabbage
> as she cuts a thousand capers
> with her milk foaming inside her as an accompaniment;
>   and—if my going to and fro
> has happened to tire me out—
> I prefer to arrange the marriage of an eggplant
> with an equal amount of bacon;
>   and, later on, a snack,
> while supper is being prepared,
> off a bunch of my own grapes hanging from the ceiling
> (may God protect the vines from hail!);

---

10. Fernán Gómez. The Knights of Calatrava were friars as well as warriors.

y cenar un salpicón
con su aceite y su pimienta,
y irme a la cama contenta,
y al «inducas tentación» *ella no vara entra su tentación*
rezalle mis devociones;
que cuantas raposerías,
con su amor y sus porfías,
tienen estos bellacones;
porque todo su cuidado,
después de darnos disgusto,
es anochecer con gusto
y amanecer con enfado.

PAS.:   Tienes, Laurencia, razón;
que en dejando de querer,
más ingratos suelen ser
que al villano el gorrión.
En el invierno, que el frío
tiene los campos helados,
decienden de los tejados,
diciéndole «tío, tío»,
hasta llegar a comer
las migajas de la mesa;
mas luego que el frío cesa
y el campo ven florecer,
no bajan diciendo «tío»,
del beneficio olvidados,
mas saltando en los tejados,
dicen: «judío, judío».
Pues tales los hombres son:
cuando nos han menester,
somos su vida, su ser,
su alma, su corazón;
pero, pasadas las ascuas,
las tías somos judías, *gran insulto no eres nombre*
y en vez de llamarnos tías,
anda el nombre de las pascuas.

and to sup on cold chopped meat
with olive oil and peppers,
and go to bed satisfied,
and say my prayers
      to God:[11]
I prefer all this to all the foxy tricks
that these rogues have,
with their love and their persistence;
      because their entire concern,
after they have done us wrong,
is to go to bed with pleasure
and get up the next morning with irritation.

PAS.:   You're right, Laurencia;
because, once they cease loving us,
they're usually more ungrateful
than the sparrows are to the peasants.

      In winter, when the cold
keeps the fields frozen,
they come down from the roofs,
saying "Uncle, Uncle,"[12]
      and they even eat
the bread crumbs off the table;
but after the cold days are over
and they see the field in blossom,
      they no longer come down saying "Uncle,"
but, forgetting the favors they have been given,
they hop on the roofs
saying "Jew, Jew."[13]
      Well, that's the way men are:
when they need us,
we're their life, their being,
their soul, their heart;
      but, when the glowing coals have died down,
the former "aunts" become "Jewesses,"
and, instead of calling us "Aunt,"
they insult us.

---

11. In the Spanish text, the name of God is replaced by macaronic Latin words from the Lord's Prayer: "lead [us not into] temptation."   12. A respectful form of address to older people in rural areas; the sound of *tío* imitates the sparrows' chirping.   13. A particularly deadly insult.

LAU.:   ¡No fiarse de ninguno!
PAS.:   Lo mismo digo, Laurencia.

              Salen MENGO *y* BARRILDO *y* FRONDOSO.

FRO.:   En aquesta diferencia
              andas, Barrildo, importuno.
BAR.:   A lo menos aquí está
              quien nos dirá lo más cierto.
MEN.:   Pues hagamos un concierto
              antes que lleguéis allá,
                 y es que, si juzgan por mí,
              me dé cada cual la prenda,
              precio de aquesta contienda.
BAR.:   Desde aquí digo que sí.
                 Mas si pierdes, ¿qué darás?
MEN.:   Daré mi rabel de boj,
              que vale más que una troj,
              porque yo le estimo en más.
BAR.:   Soy contento.
FRO.:   Pues lleguemos.
              Dios os guarde, hermosas damas.
LAU.:   ¿Damas, Frondoso, nos llamas?
FRO.:   Andar al uso queremos:
                 al bachiller, licenciado;
              al ciego, tuerto; al bisojo,
              bizco; resentido, al cojo,
              y buen hombre al descuidado;
                 al ignorante, sesudo;
              al mal galán, soldadesca;
              a la boca grande, fresca,
              y al ojo pequeño, agudo;
                 al pleitista, diligente;
              gracioso, al entremetido;
              al hablador, entendido,
              y al insufrible, valiente;
                 al cobarde, para poco;
              al atrevido, bizarro;
              compañero, al que es un jarro,

LAU.:   Don't trust a one of them!   *Men are not to be trusted*
PAS.:   That's what I say, too, Laurencia.

Enter MENGO, BARRILDO, *and* FRONDOSO.

FRO.:   In this dispute
               you're being a nuisance,[14] Barrildo.
BAR.:   At least we have here
               someone who'll give us the correct answer.
MEN.:   Then, let's make a deal
               before you two get there:
                    to wit, if their judgment is in my favor,
               that each of you pays me a forfeit,
               the prize of this contest.
BAR.:   I agree, with no further ado.
               But, if you lose, what will *you* give?
MEN.:   I'll give my boxwood rebec,
               which is worth more than a granary,
               because I value it more.
BAR.:   I'm satisfied.
FRO.:   Then, let's go up to them.
               May God keep you, lovely ladies!
LAU.:   You call us ladies, Frondoso?
FRO.:   We want to follow the fashion: A college grad
                    is addressed as a man with a master's degree;
               the blind are called one-eyed; the crosseyed   *flattery when addressing people*
               are said to squint; the lame, to have aching legs;
               and careless men are called good fellows,
                    the ignorant are called wise;
               the rough wooer is said to be soldierly,
               a large mouth is said to be tempting;
               a small eye, piercing;
                    the litigious man is called diligent;
               the meddler is called entertaining;
               the chatterbox, learned;
               and the unbearable man, valiant;
                    the coward is said to be "not much good";
               the impertinent man, gallant;
               the fool, a good companion;

14. Or: "you're in the wrong."

y desenfadado, al loco;
  gravedad, al descontento;
a la calva, autoridad;
donaire, a la necedad,
y al pie grande, buen cimiento;
  al buboso, resfriado;
comedido, al arrogante;
al ingenioso, constante;
al corcovado, cargado.
  Esto llamaros imito,
damas, sin pasar de aquí;
porque fuera hablar así
proceder en infinito.

LAU.:   Allá en la ciudad, Frondoso,
llámase por cortesía
de esa suerte; y a fe mía,
que hay otro más riguroso
  y peor vocabulario
en las lenguas descorteses.

FRO.:   Querría que lo dijeses.

LAU.:   Es todo a esotro contrario:
  al hombre grave, enfadoso;
venturoso, al descompuesto;
melancólico, al compuesto,
y al que reprehende, odioso;
  importuno, al que aconseja;
al liberal, moscatel;
al justiciero, crüel,
y al que es piadoso, madeja;
  al que es constante, villano;
al que es cortés, lisonjero;
hipócrita, al limosnero,
y pretendiente, al cristiano;
  al justo mérito, dicha;
a la verdad, imprudencia;
cobardía, a la paciencia,
y culpa, a lo que es desdicha;
  necia, a la mujer honesta;

and the madman, carefree;
　　gravity is ascribed to the malcontent;
authority, to baldness;
wit, to folly;
and big feet are said to be a firm foundation;
　　the man with a swollen nose is said to have a head cold;
the arrogant man is called reserved;
the lunatic, steady;
the hunchback, round-shouldered.
　　When I call you ladies, I imitate
this practice, but I limit myself to the above;
because, talking this way,
I could go on forever.

LAU.:　　Yonder in the city, Frondoso,
people are called such things
out of politeness; but, by my faith,
there's another set of words,
　　more severe and worse,
when the speakers are less polished.

FRO.:　　I'd like you to state it.

LAU.:　　It's just the opposite of the other one you mentioned:
　　the sedate man is called disagreeable;
the immoderate man is called lucky;[15]
the moderate man, melancholy;
and the reproachful man, hateful;
　　the man who gives advice, a nuisance;
the generous man, a spendthrift;
the justice-loving man, cruel;
and the compassionate man, a milksop;
　　the constant man, a peasant,
the courteous man, a flatterer;
the charitable man, a hypocrite;
the Christian man, an office-seeker;
　　true merit is called luck;
truth, imprudence;
patience, cowardice;
and bad luck, fault;
　　honest women are called foolish;

[handwritten margin note: In country, people don't use same words]

---

15. This doesn't make very much sense, and one editor emended the line to read: *al que es veraz, descompuesto* ("the truthful man is called immoderate").

mal hecha, a la hermosa y casta,
y a la honrada . . . Pero basta;
que esto basta por respuesta.

MEN.:   Digo que eres el dimuño.

BAR.:   ¡Soncas que lo dice mal!

MEN.:   Apostaré que la sal
la echó el cura con el puño.

LAU.:   ¿Qué contienda os ha traído
si no es que mal lo entendí?

FRO.:   Oye, por tu vida.

LAU.:   Di.

FRO.:   Préstame, Laurencia, oído.

LAU.:   ¿Cómo prestado? Y aun dado.
Desde agora os doy el mío.

FRO.:   En tu discreción confío.

LAU.:   ¿Qué es lo que habéis apostado?

FRO.:   Yo y Barrildo contra Mengo.

LAU.:   ¿Qué dice Mengo?

BAR.:   Una cosa
que, siendo cierta y forzosa,
la niega.

MEN.   A negarla vengo,
porque yo sé que es verdad.

LAU.:   ¿Qué dice?

BAR.:   Que no hay amor.

LAU.:   Generalmente, es rigor.

BAR.:   Es rigor y es necedad.
Sin amor, no se pudiera
ni aun el mundo conservar.

MEN.:   Yo no sé filosofar;
leer, ¡ojalá supiera!   — No puede leer
Pero si los elementos
en discordia eterna viven,
y de los mismos reciben
nuestros cuerpos alimentos,
cólera y melancolía,
flema y sangre, claro está.

BAR.:   El mundo de acá y de allá,
Mengo, todo es armonía.

	good-looking and chaste women are called misshapen;
	and respectable women . . . But enough;
	because this is enough for an answer.
MEN.:	I say you're the Devil!
BAR.:	My, but she's got a sharp tongue!
MEN.:	I'll bet that the priest
	tossed salt on her by the fistful![16]
LAU.:	What dispute brought you here,
	if I didn't hear you incorrectly?
FRO.:	By your life, hear me out.
LAU.:	Speak.
FRO.:	Laurencia, lend me your ears.
LAU.:	Why lend? Why not give?
	From here on, I give you mine.
FRO.:	I'm relying on your good sense.
LAU.:	What wager have you made?
FRO.:	It's me and Barrildo against Mengo.
LAU.:	What does Mengo say?
BAR.:	There's something
	that, even though it's necessarily true,
	he denies.
MEN.:	I deny it
	because I know I'm in the right.
LAU.:	What does he say?
BAR.:	That there's no such thing as love.
LAU.:	Stated so categorically, it's an extreme viewpoint.
BAR.:	It's extreme, and it's foolishness.
	Without love, the world itself
	couldn't go on existing.
MEN.:	I'm not skilled in philosophy,
	I wish I could even read!
	But, if the elements
	live in eternal discord,
	and if it's from them that
	our bodies receive nourishment—
	choler and melancholy,
	phlegm and sanguinity—the case is clear.
BAR.:	The world of earth and heaven,
	Mengo, is all harmony.

---

16. Salt was sprinkled on an infant being christened (and "salt" is a term for wit).

Armonía es puro amor,
porque el amor es concierto.

MEN.:   Del natural os advierto
que yo no niego el valor.
    Amor hay, y el que entre sí
gobierna todas las cosas,
correspondencias forzosas
de cuanto se mira aquí;
    y yo jamás he negado
que cada cual tiene amor
correspondiente a su humor,
que le conserva en su estado.
    Mi mano al golpe que viene
mi cara defenderá;
mi pie, huyendo, estorbará
el daño que el cuerpo tiene.
    Cerraránse mis pestañas,
si al ojo le viene mal,
porque es amor natural.

PAS.:   Pues ¿de qué nos desengañas?

MEN.:   De que nadie tiene amor
más que a su misma persona.

PAS.:   Tú mientes, Mengo, y perdona;
porque ¿es materia el rigor
    con que un hombre a una mujer,
o un animal quiere y ama
su semejante?

MEN.:   Eso llama
amor propio, y no querer.
    ¿Qué es amor?

LAU.:   Es un deseo
de hermosura.

MEN.:   Esa hermosura
¿por qué el amor la procura?

LAU.:   Para gozarla.

MEN.:   Eso creo.
    Pues ese gusto que intenta,
¿no es para él mismo?

LAU.:   Es así.

MEN.:   Luego, ¿por quererse a sí
busca el bien que le contenta?

              Harmony is pure love,
           because love is agreement.
MEN.:   I point out that I don't deny
           the existence of natural love.
              Love exists, the kind that governs
           the interrelationships of all things,
           the necessary interchanges
           of all the things that we observe;
              and I have never denied
           that each one of us possesses a love
           that corresponds to his own bodily humor,
           and which maintains his own character and condition.
              My hand will protect my face
           from a coming blow;
           by running away, my foot will avoid
           an injury to my body.
              My eyelids will close
           if harm threatens my eyes:
           that is natural love.
PAS.:   And so, what illusion are you ridding us of?
MEN.:   I'm proving that nobody loves
           anything but his own self.
PAS.:   That's a lie, Mengo, excuse me!
           Because: is the vehemence
              with which a man loves a woman
           or an animal loves and desires
           its mate, merely a physical instinct?
MEN.:   Call that
           self-love, not affection.
              What is love?
LAU.:   It's a thirst   *the Symposium*
           for beauty.
MEN.:   And this beauty,
           why does love seek it?
LAU.:   To enjoy it.
MEN.:   That's just what I believe.
              Well, that pleasure it's after,
           isn't it for itself?
LAU.:   That's right.
MEN.:   Well then, because it loves itself
           it seeks the good things in which it delights?

LAU.:   Es verdad.

MEN.:   Pues de ese modo
no hay amor, sino el que digo,
que por mi gusto le sigo,
y quiero dármele en todo.

BAR.:   Dijo el cura del lugar
cierto día en el sermón
que había cierto Platón
que nos enseñaba a amar;
            que éste amaba el alma sola
y la virtud de lo amado.

PAS.:   En materia habéis entrado
que, por ventura, acrisola
            los caletres de los sabios
en sus cademias y escuelas.

LAU.:   Muy bien dice, y no te muelas
en persuadir sus agravios.
            Da gracias, Mengo, a los cielos,
que te hicieron sin amor.

MEN.:   ¿Amas tú?

LAU.:   Mi propio honor.

FRO.:   Dios te castigue con celos.

BAR.:   ¿Quién gana?

PAS.:   Con la quistión
podéis ir al sacristán,
porque él o el cura os darán
bastante satisfación.
            Laurencia no quiere bien,
yo tengo poca experiencia:
¿cómo daremos sentencia?

FRO.:   ¿Qué mayor que ese desdén?

                Sale FLORES.

FLO.:   Dios guarde a la buena gente.

PAS.:   Este es del comendador
crïado.

LAU.:   ¡Gentil azor!
¿De adónde bueno, pariente?

FLO.:   ¿No me veis a lo soldado?

LAU.:   ¿Viene don Fernando acá?

FLO.:   La guerra se acaba ya,

LAU.:   That's true.
MEN.:   Well, if that's the case,
the only love that exists is the one I'm talking about,
which I pursue for my pleasure,
and which I want to enjoy in everything I do.
BAR.:   Our village priest said
in his sermon one day
that there was once a certain Plato *[Mrc drop] [walks out]*
who taught us the right way to love;
for he loved only the soul
and the virtue of the beloved object.
PAS.:   You've entered onto a topic
that perhaps tests
the wits of scholars
in their 'cademies and schools.
LAU.:   She speaks very truly, so don't wear yourself out
refuting his offensive remarks.
Mengo, thank the heavens
for having created you lacking in love.
MEN.:   Are you in love?
LAU.:   With my own honor.
FRO.:   May God punish you by making you jealous!
BAR.:   Who's the winner?
PAS.:   You can take the problem
to the sacristan,
because he or the priest will give you
a sufficient explanation.
Laurencia isn't in love with anyone,
and I don't have much experience:
how can we pronounce judgment?
FRO.:   What harsher judgment can there be than this contempt?

Enter FLORES.

FLO.:   May God keep you good people.
PAS.:   This is one of the Commander's
servants.
LAU.:   A pleasant bird of prey!
What fine wind brings you, friend?
FLO.:   Don't you see I'm in military dress?
LAU.:   Is Don Fernando coming here?
FLO.:   The war is now over, *[?]*

puesto que nos ha costado
alguna sangre y amigos.

FRO.: Contadnos cómo pasó.

FLO.: ¿Quién lo dirá como yo,
siendo mis ojos testigos?
Para emprender la jornada
de esta ciudad, que ya tiene
nombre de Ciudad Real,
juntó el gallardo maestre
dos mil lucidos infantes
de sus vasallos valientes
y trecientos de a caballo
de seglares y de freiles;
porque la cruz roja obliga
cuantos al pecho la tienen,
aunque sean de orden sacro;
mas contra moros, se entiende.
Salió el muchacho bizarro
con una casaca verde,
bordada de cifras de oro,
que sólo los brazaletes
por las mangas descubrían,
que seis alamares prenden.
Un corpulento bridón,
rucio rodado, que al Betis
bebió el agua, y en su orilla
despuntó la grama fértil;
el codón labrado en cintas
de ante, y el rizo copete
cogido en blancas lazadas,
que con las moscas de nieve
que bañan la blanca piel
iguales labores teje.
A su lado Fernán Gómez,
vuestro señor, en un fuerte
melado, de negros cabos,
puesto que con blanco bebe.
Sobre turca jacerina,
peto y espaldar luciente,
con naranjada casaca,
que de oro y perlas guarnece;
el morrión que, coronado

	though it has cost us
	some blood and friends.
FRO.:	Tell us how things went.
FLO.:	Who could give you a better report than I can,

FRO.:   Tell us how things went.

FLO.:   Who could give you a better report than I can,

since I was an eyewitness?
    To undertake the expedition
to that city, which now bears
the name Ciudad Real, the King's City,
the gallant Master assembled
two thousand splendid foot soldiers
from among his brave vassals
and three hundred cavalrymen,
some of them laymen and some of them friars;
because the red Cross obligates
all who wear it on their breast,
even if they have taken holy orders;
but against Moors, of course.
The dashing lad sallied forth
in a green surcoat
embroidered with golden monograms,
only his brassarts
showing through his sleeves,
which were fastened by six braid buttons.
A stout saddled charger,
a dapple gray, which drank the water
of the Guadalquivir, and on its banks
cropped the luxuriant grass;
its tail covering worked with straps
of buckskin, and its curling mane
tied up with white bows,
so that it resembled woven cloth
matching the "flies on snow"
that sprinkled its white hide.
By his side, Fernán Gómez,
your lord, on a strong
honey-colored horse with black feet and mane,
though it drinks through a white muzzle.
Over his Turkish coat of mail,
a gleaming breast- and backplate,
with an orange surcoat
adorned with gold and pearls;
his helmet, crowned

con blancas plumas, parece
que del color naranjado
aquellos azares vierte;
ceñida al brazo una liga
roja y blanca, con que mueve
un fresno entero por lanza,
que hasta en Granada le temen.
La ciudad se puso en arma;
dicen que salir no quieren
de la corona real,
y el patrimonio defienden.
Entróla, bien resistida,
y el maestre a los rebeldes
y a los que entonces trataron
su honor injuriosamente,
mandó cortar las cabezas,
y a los de la baja plebe,
con mordazas en la boca,
azotar públicamente.
Queda en ella tan temido
y tan amado, que creen
que quien en tan pocos años
pelea, castiga y vence,
ha de ser en otra edad
rayo del África fértil,
que tantas lunas azules
a su roja cruz sujete.
Al comendador y a todos
ha hecho tantas mercedes,
que el saco de la ciudad
el de su hacienda parece.
Mas ya la música suena:
recebilde alegremente,
que al triunfo, las voluntades
son los mejores laureles.

Sale el COMENDADOR *y* ORTUÑO; MÚSICOS, JUAN ROJO,
y ESTEBAN, ALONSO, ALCALDES.

MÚS.:   *Sea bienvenido*
el comendadore

with white plumes, seemed
to be producing white orange blossoms
from the orange coat;
a red and white ribbon
girding his arm, with which he brandished
a whole ash trunk as a lance,
so that he is feared even in Granada.
The city armed itself;
they said they refused to abandon
the royal crown,
and that they'd defend their patrimony.
Despite strong resistance, the Master entered
the city, and ordered that the rebels,
and those who were then
insulting his honor,
be beheaded,
and those of the lower classes
be gagged
and publicly whipped.
He remains there, so greatly feared
and loved that it is the general belief
that a person so young
who can fight, punish, and conquer
will surely be, when he is older,
a scourge of fertile Africa,
and will make many blue Crescents
submit to his red Cross.
To the Commander and all the rest
he has made so many gifts
that the sacking of the city
is like that of his personal property.
But the music is already playing:
welcome the Commander cheerfully,
for at a time of triumph, people's good wills
are the best laurels.

Enter the COMMANDER, ORTUÑO, MUSICIANS, JUAN ROJO,
and the joint mayors ESTEBAN *and* ALONSO.

MUS.:   "Welcome
            to the Commander,

de rendir las tierras
y matar los hombres.
¡Vivan los Guzmanes!
¡Vivan los Girones!
Si en las paces blando,
dulce en las razones.
Venciendo moricos
fuerte como un roble,
de Ciudad Reale
viene vencedore;
que a Fuenteovejuna
trae los sus pendones.
¡Viva muchos años,
viva Fernán Gómez!

COM.:   Villa, yo os agradezco justamente
el amor que me habéis aquí mostrado.

ALO.:   Aun no muestra una parte del que siente.
Pero ¿qué mucho que seáis amado,
mereciéndolo vos?

EST.:   Fuenteovejuna
y el regimiento que hoy habéis honrado,
que recibáis os ruega y importuna
un pequeño presente, que esos carros
traen, señor, no sin vergüenza alguna,
de voluntades y árboles bizarros,
más que de ricos dones. Lo primero
traen dos cestas de polidos barros;
de gansos viene un ganadillo entero,
que sacan por las redes las cabezas,
para cantar vueso valor guerrero.
Diez cebones en sal, valientes piezas,
sin otras menudencias y cecinas;
y más que guantes de ámbar, sus cortezas.
Cien pares de capones y gallinas,
que han dejado vïudos a sus gallos
en las aldeas que miráis vecinas.
Acá no tienen armas ni caballos,
no jaeces bordados de oro puro,
si no es oro el amor de los vasallos.
Y porque digo puro, os aseguro
que vienen doce cueros, que aun en cueros

who has subjected lands
and killed men!
Long live the Guzmán family!
Long live the Girón family!
If he is gentle in peacetime
and softly spoken,
when conquering Moors
he is sturdy as an oak.
From Ciudad Real
he arrives as a conqueror;
back to Fuenteovejuna
he bears his banners.
May he live many years,
long live Fernán Gómez!"

COM.:   Townspeople, it is only right for me to thank you
for the love you have shown me here.

ALO.:   And yet the town is showing only a part of what it feels.
But, what wonder is it that you are loved,
seeing that you deserve it?

EST.:   Fuenteovejuna,
and the town council, whom you have honored today,
ask and beg you to accept
a small gift, which these carts
bear, my lord, though we are somewhat shamefaced,
since our good wishes and our decorated poles are splendid,
but our presents aren't costly. First of all,
they're bringing you two basketfuls of polished earthenware;
next comes an entire flock of geese
poking their heads through the netting
to sing of your martial valor.
Ten salted hogs, fine specimens,
not to mention other offals and cured meat;
the rinds smell better than gloves scented with ambergris.
A hundred pairs of capons and hens,
who have left their roosters widowed
in the villages you see nearby.
Here the people don't have armor or horses,
or horse trappings embroidered with pure gold,
unless the love of your vassals counts as gold.
And, since I'm speaking plainly, I assure you
that twelve wineskins are coming, such that even

por enero podéis guardar un muro,
  si de ellos aforráis vuestros guerreros,
mejor que de las armas aceradas;
que el vino suele dar lindos aceros.
  De quesos y otras cosas no excusadas
no quiero daros cuenta: justo pecho
de voluntades que tenéis ganadas;
y a vos y a vuestra casa, buen provecho.

COM.:   Estoy muy agradecido.
  Id, regimiento, en buen hora.

ALO.:   Descansad, señor, agora,
y seáis muy bien venido;
  que esa espadaña que veis
y juncia, a vuestros umbrales,
fueran perlas orientales,
y mucho más merecéis,
  a ser posible a la villa.

COM.:   Así lo creo, señores.
Id con Dios.

EST.:   Ea, cantores,
vaya otra vez la letrilla.

MÚS.:   *Sea bienvenido*
el comendadore
de rendir las tierras
y matar los hombres . . .

                     Vanse.

COM.:   Esperad vosotras dos.
LAU.:   ¿Qué manda su señoría?
COM.:   ¿Desdenes el otro día,
pues, conmigo? ¡Bien, por Dios!
LAU.:   ¿Habla contigo, Pascuala?
PAS.:   Conmigo no, tirte ahuera.
COM.:   Con vos hablo, hermosa fiera,
y con esotra zagala.
  ¿Mías no sois?
PAS.:   Sí, señor;
mas no para cosas tales.
COM.:   Entrad, pasad los umbrales;
hombres hay, no hayáis temor.

in your own bare skins you can guard a wall in January,
    if you line your soldiers' bellies with their contents,
more warmly than in steel armor;
because wine is apt to steel men's hearts.
    Of the cheeses and other not unneedful things
I won't give you a detailed account: it is a fair tribute
from the good will you have won;
and may you and your household enjoy them all!

COM.:   I'm very grateful.
    Depart, councilmen, with my best wishes.

ALO.:   Now rest, my lord,
you are most welcome;
    these bulrushes that you see,
and these sedges spread over your threshold,
would be orient pearls
(for you deserve much more)
    if the town could afford it.

COM.:   I take you at your word, gentlemen.
    Go with God.

EST.:   Hey, singers,
let's have the refrain again!

MUS.:   "Welcome
to the Commander,
who has subjected lands
and killed men! . . ."

Exit [all but the two girls, and the COMMANDER *and his servants].*

COM.:   You two, wait.

LAU.:   What does Your Lordship command?

COM.:   So, you were standoffish
with me the other day? A fine thing, by God!

LAU.:   Is he talking to you, Pascuala?

PAS.:   Not to me. Come off it!

COM.:   I'm talking to *you*, my wild beauty,
and to this other girl.
    Don't you both belong to me?

PAS.:   Yes, my lord,
but not for such purposes. *Ah! bet 'em, girl!*

COM.:   Come in, cross the threshold;
there are people inside, don't be afraid.

LAU.:   Si los alcaldes entraran,
            que de uno soy hija yo,
            bien huera entrar, mas si no . . .
COM.:   Flores . . .
FLO.:   Señor . . .
COM.:   ¿Qué reparan
            en no hacer lo que les digo?
FLO.:   Entrá, pues.
LAU.:   No nos agarre.
FLO.:   Entrad; que sois necias.
PAS.:   Harre;
            que echaréis luego el postigo.
FLO.:   Entrad, que os quiere enseñar
            lo que trae de la guerra.
COM.:   Si entraren, Ortuño, cierra.
LAU.:   Flores, dejadnos pasar.
ORT.:   ¡También venís presentadas
            con lo demás!
PAS.:   ¡Bien a fe!
            Desvíese, no le dé . . .
FLO.:   Basta; que son extremadas.
LAU.:   ¿No basta a vueso señor
            tanta carne presentada?
ORT.:   La vuestra es la que le agrada.
LAU.:   Reviente de mal dolor.

                        Vanse.

FLO.:   ¡Muy buen recado llevamos!
            No se ha de poder sufrir
            lo que nos ha de decir
            cuando sin ellas nos vamos.
ORT.:   Quien sirve se obliga a esto:
            si en algo desea medrar,
            o con paciencia ha de estar,
            o ha de despedirse presto.

        Vanse los dos, y salgan el rey don FERNANDO,
    la reina doña ISABEL, MANRIQUE *y acompañamiento.*

ISA.:   Digo, señor, que conviene
            el no haber descuido en esto,

LAU.:	If the mayors had gone in,
	since I'm the daughter of one of them,
	it would be all right for me, too; but otherwise . . .
COM.:	Flores!
FLO.:	My lord?
COM.:	Why do they insist
	on disobeying my orders?
FLO.:	Get in, then.
LAU.:	Don't grab us.
FLO.:	Get in; you're acting foolish.
PAS.:	Nothing doing,
	because you'll shut the wicket on us.
FLO.:	Go in; he wants to show you
	what he brought back from the war.
COM.:	If they go in, Ortuño, lock the door. [*Exit.*]
LAU.:	Flores, let us pass.
ORT.:	You're also here as presents
	just like the rest!
PAS.:	Is that the truth?!
	If he doesn't move out of the way, I'll give him . . .
FLO.:	Enough! They're too hotheaded.
LAU.:	Isn't your master satisfied
	with all the meat given to him?
ORT.:	The meat he's after is yours.
LAU.:	I hope he gets sick and bursts!

Exit [the girls].

FLO.:	We're bringing a fine message!
	We won't be able to stand
	the things he'll surely say to us
	when we go in without them.
ORT.:	Every servant finds this unavoidable:
	if he wishes to prosper in any affair,
	he either must have patience
	or else he has to resign right away.

Exit. Enter KING FERNANDO [*Ferdinand*],
QUEEN ISABEL [*Isabella*], MANRIQUE, *and retinue.*

ISA.:	I say, my lord, that it's expedient
	not to be negligent in this matter,

por ver Alfonso en tal puesto,
y su ejército previene.
    Y es bien ganar por la mano
antes que el daño veamos;
que si no lo remediamos,
el ser muy cierto está llano.

REY: De Navarra y de Aragón
está el socorro seguro,
y de Castilla procuro
hacer la reformación,
    de modo que el buen suceso
con la prevención se vea.

ISA.:   Pues vuestra majestad crea
que el buen fin consiste en eso.

MAN.:   Aguardando tu licencia
dos regidores están,
de Ciudad Real: ¿entrarán?

REY: No les nieguen mi presencia.

Salen dos REGIDORES *de Ciudad Real.*

REG. 1.º: Católico rey Fernando,
a quien ha enviado el cielo
desde Aragón a Castilla,
para bien y amparo nuestro:
en nombre de Ciudad Real
a vuestro valor supremo
humildes nos presentamos,
el real amparo pidiendo.
A mucha dicha tuvimos
tener título de vuestros;
pero pudo derribarnos
de este honor el hado adverso.
El famoso don Rodrigo
Téllez Girón, cuyo esfuerzo
es en valor extremado,
aunque es en la edad tan tierno,
maestre de Calatrava,
él, ensanchar pretendiendo
el honor de la encomienda,
nos puso apretado cerco.

since we see Alfonso in such a good position,
preparing his army.
   It's a good thing to take the first step
before we find ourselves harmed;
because, unless we remedy the matter,
that will clearly come to pass.

KING: From Navarre and Aragon
we are sure of aid,
and in Castile I am trying
to bring about political reform,
   so that good results
can be obtained by foresight.

ISA.:   Your Majesty should be sure
that a successful conclusion is based on such measures.

MAN.:   Awaiting your word of admittance
are two councilmen
from Ciudad Real. Shall they come in?

KING: Let my presence not be denied them.

Enter two COUNCILMEN *from Ciudad Real.*

COU. 1:   Catholic King Fernando,
whom heaven has sent
from Aragon to Castile
for our benefit and protection:
in the name of Ciudad Real
we humbly present ourselves
to your supreme merit,
requesting royal protection.
We counted it great good fortune
to be called your subjects;
but adverse fate was able
to topple us from that honor.
The celebrated Don Rodrigo
Téllez Girón, whose efforts
in deeds of valor are outstanding
though he is of such tender years,
he, the Master of Calatrava,
attempting to increase
the honor of his military order,
laid close siege to us.

Con valor nos prevenimos,
a su fuerza resistiendo,
tanto, que arroyos corrían
de la sangre de los muertos.
Tomó posesión, en fin,
pero no llegara a hacerlo,
a no le dar Fernán Gómez
orden, ayuda y consejo.
Él queda en la posesión,
y sus vasallos seremos,
suyos, a nuestro pesar,
a no remediarlo presto.

REY: ¿Dónde queda Fernán Gómez?

REG. 1.º: En Fuenteovejuna creo,
por ser su villa, y tener
en ella casa y asiento.
Allí, con más libertad
de la que decir podemos,
tiene a los súbditos suyos
de todo contento ajenos.

REY: ¿Tenéis algún capitán?

REG. 2.º: Señor, el no haberle es cierto,
pues no escapó ningún noble
de preso, herido o de muerto.

ISA.:   Ese caso no requiere
ser despacio remediado,
que es dar al contrario osado
el mismo valor que adquiere;
        y puede el de Portugal,
hallando puerta segura,
entrar por Extremadura
y causarnos mucho mal.

REY: Don Manrique, partid luego,
llevando dos compañías;
remediad sus demasías,
sin darles ningún sosiego.
        El conde de Cabra ir puede
con vos, que es Córdoba osado,

We took precautions bravely,
resisting his force,
to such an extent that streams of blood
flowed from the dead.
Finally he captured the city,
but he wouldn't have succeeded in doing so
had not Fernán Gómez given him
instructions, assistance, and advice.
He remains in possession,
and we will be his vassals,
his, to our regret,
unless things are rectified quickly.

KING: Where is Fernán Gómez at the moment?

COU. 1: In Fuenteovejuna, I believe,
because that's in his domain and he has
house and domicile there.
There, with greater license
than we could possibly tell,
he deprives his subjects
of all pleasure in life.

KING: Do you have any military leader?

COU. 2: Sire, I'm sure there is none,
because no nobleman has avoided
being captured, wounded, or killed.

ISA.: This situation requires
no tardy relief,
or else we'll give our bold adversary
the full benefit that his valor has won;
and the king of Portugal,
finding a safe entranceway,
will be able to invade Extremadura
and cause us great damage.

KING: Don Manrique,[17] leave at once,
taking two companies with you;
repair their outrages
and give them no rest.
The count of Cabra[18] can go
with you, because Córdoba is bold

---

17. Rodrigo Manrique, Master of Santiago; on the occasion of his death, his son Jorge Manrique wrote one of the most famous poems in the Spanish language. 18. Diego Fernández de Córdoba (called Córdoba in the next line).

a quien nombre de soldado
todo el mundo le concede;
    que éste es el medio mejor
que la ocasión nos ofrece.

MAN.:   El acuerdo me parece
como de tan gran valor.
    Pondré límite a su exceso,
si el vivir en mí no cesa.

ISA.:   Partiendo vos a la empresa,
seguro está el buen suceso.

Vanse todos y salen LAURENCIA *y* FRONDOSO.

LAU.:   A medio torcer los paños,
quise, atrevido Frondoso,
para no dar qué decir,
desviarme del arroyo;
decir a tus demasías
que murmura el pueblo todo
que me miras y te miro,
y todos nos traen sobre ojo.
Y como tú eres zagal
de los que huellan, brïoso,
y excediendo a los demás,
vistes bizarro y costoso,
en todo el lugar no hay moza,
o mozo en el prado o soto,
que no se afirme diciendo
que ya para en uno somos;
y esperan todos el día
que el sacristán Juan Chamorro
nos eche de la tribuna,
en dejando los piporros.
Y mejor sus trojes vean
de rubio trigo en agosto
atestadas y colmadas,
y sus tinajas de mosto,
que tal imaginación
me ha llegado a dar enojo:
ni me desvela ni aflige,
ni en ella el cuidado pongo.

and everyone grants him
the name of good soldier;
   since these are the best means
that opportunity offers us.

MAN.:   The plan seems to me
to be of great merit.
   I shall set limits to his excesses,
if I remain alive.

ISA.:   With you departing on this enterprise,
good results are assured.

All exit. Enter LAURENCIA *and* FRONDOSO.

LAU.;   Halfway through wringing out the laundry,
bold Frondoso, I decided
to leave the stream
so as not to lend fuel to gossip;
and to tell you you're going too far,
and the whole town is whispering
about your having your eye on me, and me on you,
and everybody is observing us.
And since you're one of those boys
who are high-spirited and independent,
and you outdo all the rest,
dressing in fancy, expensive clothes,
there isn't a girl in the whole place
or a young fellow in the meadow or the thicket
who doesn't feel justified in saying
that we're as good as married;
and everyone is waiting for the day
when the sacristan Juan Chamorro,
leaving aside his bassoon music,
calls our names from the choirloft.
But better that our neighbors should see their granaries
filled and crammed
with red wheat in August,
and their vats filled with new wine,
than that their supposition about us
should succeed in vexing me!
It doesn't keep me up at night, it doesn't grieve me,
and I pay no mind to it.

FRO.:   Tal me tienen tus desdenes,
         bella Laurencia, que tomo,
         en el peligro de verte,
         la vida, cuando te oigo.
         Si sabes que es mi intención
         el desear ser tu esposo,
         mal premio das a mi fe.
LAU.:   Es que yo no sé dar otro.
FRO.:   ¿Posible es que no te duelas
         de verme tan cuidadoso,
         y que, imaginando en ti,
         ni bebo, duermo ni como?
         ¿Posible es tanto rigor
         en ese angélico rostro?
         ¡Viven los cielos que rabio!
LAU.:   Pues salúdate, Frondoso.   "Take care of yourself"
FRO.:   Ya te pido yo salud,
         y que ambos, como palomos,
         estemos, juntos los picos,
         con arrullos sonorosos,
         después de darnos la iglesia . . .
LAU.:   Dilo a mi tío Juan Rojo;
         que aunque no te quiero bien,   aceptas
         ya tengo algunos asomos.   Frondoso
FRO.:   ¡Ay de mí! El señor es este.
LAU.:   Tirando viene a algún corzo.
         Escóndete en esas ramas.
FRO.:   ¡Y con qué celos me escondo!

                Sale el COMENDADOR.

COM.:   No es malo venir siguiendo
         un corcillo temeroso
         y topar tan bella gama.
LAU.:   Aquí descansaba un poco
         de haber lavado unos paños;
         y así, al arroyo me torno,
         si manda su señoría.
COM.:   Aquesos desdenes toscos

FRO.:   Your disdain, beautiful Laurencia,
         has put me in such a state that,
         at the perilous moment of seeing you,
         I risk my life[19] when I hear you.
         If you know that my goal
         is wishing to be your husband,
         you ill reward my faithfulness.

LAU.:   It's because I have no other reward to give.

FRO.:   Is it possible that you don't grieve
         to see me so full of cares
         that, when I think of you,
         I don't drink, sleep, or eat?
         Is such severity consistent
         with such an angelic face?
         By heaven, I'm rabid!

LAU.:   Then take steps to cure yourself, Frondoso.

FRO.:   I'm asking you to cure me,
         so that the two of us, like ringdoves,
         can join our beaks
         and coo noisily
         after the Church has given us . . .

LAU.:   Tell it to my uncle, Juan Rojo;
         because, even though I'm not in love with you,
         I already feel a slight inclination that way.

FRO.;   Woe is me! Our lord is here.

LAU.:   He's come this way to hunt some roebuck.
         Hide in these branches.

FRO.:   And how jealous I am as I hide!

Enter the COMMANDER.

COM.:   It's not a bad thing to be pursuing
         a timorous young roebuck,
         and to come across such a beautiful fallow-deer doe.

LAU.:   I was resting a little here
         after washing some clothes;
         and so, I'll go back to the stream
         with Your Lordship's leave.

COM.:   These rude refusals,

---

19. Another annotator says: "I regain my life."

> afrentan, bella Laurencia,
> las gracias que el poderoso
> cielo te dio, de tal suerte
> que vienes a ser un monstro.
> Mas si otras veces pudiste
> huïr mi ruego amoroso,
> agora no quiere el campo,
> amigo secreto y solo;
> que tú sola no has de ser
> tan soberbia que tu rostro
> huyas al señor que tienes,
> teniéndome a mí en tan poco.
> ¿No se rindió Sebastiana,
> mujer de Pedro Redondo,
> con ser casadas entrambas,
> y la de Martín del Pozo,
> habiendo apenas pasado
> dos días del desposorio?

LAU.:   Esas, señor, ya tenían
> de haber andado con otros
> el camino de agradaros,
> porque también muchos mozos
> merecieron sus favores.
> Id con Dios tras vueso corzo;
> que a no veros con la cruz,
> os tuviera por demonio,
> pues tanto me perseguís.

COM.:   ¡Qué estilo tan enfadoso!
> Pongo la ballesta en tierra,
> y a la prática de manos
> reduzgo melindres.

LAU.:   ¡Cómo!
> ¿Eso hacéis? ¿Estáis en vos?

Sale FRONDOSO *y toma la ballesta.*

COM.:   No te defiendas.

FRO.:   Si tomo
> la ballesta, ¡vive el cielo
> que no la ponga en el hombro!

COM.:   Acaba, ríndete.

beautiful Laurencia, are an insult
to the graces that mighty
heaven bestowed on you, and they
make you into a monster.
But, if on other occasions you were able
to flee from my request for love,
now you are prevented by being out in the fields,
which are secret and solitary friends;
for you mustn't be the only woman
so haughty that you turn your face
away from your lord and master,
showing your low opinion of me.
Didn't Sebastiana yield to me,
the wife of Pedro Redondo,
and, even though *she* was married as well,
the wife of Martín del Pozo,
scarcely two days
after their betrothal?

LAU.:   My lord, those two must have already
followed the path to your pleasure
with other men,
because many more fellows
earned their favors.
Go with God and pursue your roebuck;
because if I didn't see that Cross on you,
I'd take you for a devil,
since you persecute me so.

COM.:   What an irritating manner!
I'm laying my crossbow on the ground,
and with the force of my hands
I'll make you get over your fussiness!

LAU.:   What!
You'd do that? Are you in your right mind?

Enter FRONDOSO, *who picks up the crossbow.*

COM.:   Don't defend yourself.

FRO.:   If I've picked up
the crossbow, by heaven,
I won't just hang it over my shoulder!

COM.:   Enough! Give in!

LAU.:   ¡Cielos,
ayudadme agora!
COM.:   Solos
estamos; no tengas miedo.
FRO.:   Comendador generoso,
dejad la moza, o creed
que de mi agravio y enojo
será blanco vuestro pecho,
aunque la cruz me da asombro.
COM.:   ¡Perro villano! . . .
FRO.:   ¡No hay perro!
Huye, Laurencia.
LAU.:   Frondoso,
mira lo que haces.
FRO.:   Vete.

                    Vase.

COM.:   ¡Oh, mal haya el hombre loco
que se desciñe la espada!
Que de no espantar medroso
la caza, me la quité.
FRO.:   Pues, pardiez, señor, si toco
la nuez, que os he de apiolar.
COM.:   Ya es ida. Infame, alevoso,
suelta la ballesta luego.
Suéltala, villano.
FRO.:   ¿Cómo?
Que me quitaréis la vida.
Y advertid que amor es sordo,
y que no escucha palabras
el día que está en su trono.
COM.:   Pues, ¿la espalda ha de volver
un hombre tan valeroso
a un villano? Tira, infame,
tira y guárdate, que rompo
las leyes de caballero.
FRO.:   Eso no. Yo me conformo
con mi estado, y pues me es
guardar la vida forzoso,
con la ballesta me voy.

LAU.:   Heaven,
help me now!
COM.:   We're
alone; don't be afraid.
FRO.:   Noble Commander,
let the girl go, or, trust me,
your breast will be the target
of my affront and anger,
even though the Cross on it inspires respect.
COM.:   Peasant dog! . . .
FRO.:   There's no dog here!
Run away, Laurencia!
LAU.:   Frondoso,
take care what you do!
FRO.:   Go!

Exit [LAURENCIA].

COM.:   Oh, damn the man mad enough
to ungird his sword!
Because, in fear I'd scare away
the game, I took it off.
FRO.:   Well, by God, sir, if I release
the catch, it will be the death of you.
COM.:   She's gone now. Wretch, traitor,
drop the crossbow at once!
Drop it, peasant!
FRO.:   What?
You'd take my life.
And please note that Love is deaf
and doesn't listen to words
on days when he sits on his throne.
COM.:   So, then, a man as brave as I am
is to turn his back in retreat
on a peasant? Shoot, wretch,
shoot and stand on your guard, because I'm going to violate
the laws of chivalry.
FRO.:   Don't do that. I accept
my rank in society, and since I'm
obliged to protect my life,
I'm leaving with the crossbow.   [*Exit.*]

COM.:   ¡Peligro extraño y notorio!
          Mas yo tomaré venganza
          del agravio y del estorbo.
          ¡Que no cerrara con él!
          ¡Vive el cielo, que me corro!

Frondoso

COM.: Strange and noteworthy peril!
But I'll take vengeance
on the affront and the disturbance.
Why didn't I grapple with him?
By heaven, I feel ashamed!

Acto segundo

Salen ESTEBAN *y* REGIDOR.

EST.:   Así tenga salud, como parece,
que no se saque más agora el pósito.
El año apunta mal, y el tiempo crece,
y es mejor que el sustento esté en depósito,
aunque lo contradicen más de trece.

REG.:   Yo siempre he sido, al fin, de este propósito,
en gobernar en paz esta república.

EST.:   Hagamos de ello a Fernán Gómez súplica.
No se puede sufrir que estos astrólogos
en las cosas futuras, y ignorantes,
nos quieran persuadir con largos prólogos
los secretos a Dios sólo importantes.
¡Bueno es que, presumiendo de teólogos,
hagan un tiempo el que después y antes!
Y pidiendo el presente lo importante,
al más sabio veréis más ignorante.
    ¿Tienen ellos las nubes en su casa
y el proceder de las celestes lumbres?
¿Por dónde ven lo que en el cielo pasa,
para darnos con ello pesadumbres?
Ellos en el sembrar nos ponen tasa:
daca el trigo, cebada y las legumbres,
calabazas, pepinos y mostazas . . .

54

Act Two

Enter ESTEBAN *and a* COUNCILMAN.[20]

EST.:   As I wish for good health!—it's my feeling
          that no more grain should be withdrawn from emergency storage.
          It looks like a bad year, and the days are already growing longer,
          so that it's better for our food supply to remain locked away,
          even though more than thirteen people say the opposite.

COU.:   After all, I've always been of the same opinion,
          striving to govern this municipality peacefully.

EST.:   Let's petition Fernán Gómez on this subject.
              It's insufferable to have these astrologers
          who look into the future, ignorant as they are,
          try to convince us, in long preambles,
          of secrets to which God alone is privy.
          A fine thing, when, passing themselves off as theologians,
          they jumble past and future together!
          When present circumstances require an important decision,
          you'll find that the most learned among them is the most ignorant.
              Do they have the clouds at home,
          or the procession of the heavenly bodies?
          How can they see what's going on in heaven,
          so they can grieve us with their findings?
          At planting time they set us tax rates:
          hand over your wheat, barley, and vegetables,
          pumpkins, cucumbers, and mustard . . .

---

20. In standard Spanish editions this character is labeled "1st Councilman," even though he is the only one present. Most likely, this was intended to distinguish him from the "councilman" who appears later in the act, and who is surely Juan Rojo, Laurencia's uncle. To avoid confusion, this Dover edition calls the man in this opening scene (who is addressed as Cuadrado in Act Three) merely "Councilman," and the one later on "Juan Rojo."

Ellos son, a la fe, las calabazas.
Luego cuentan que muere una cabeza,
y después viene a ser en Trasilvania;
que el vino será poco, y la cerveza
sobrará por las partes de Alemania;
que se helará en Gascuña la cereza,
y que habrá muchos tigres en Hircania.
Y al cabo, ya se siembre o no se siembre,
el año se remata por diciembre.

Salen el licenciado LEONELO *y* BARRILDO.

LEO.:   A fe que no ganéis la palmatoria,
porque ya está ocupado el mentidero.
BAR.:   ¿Cómo os fue en Salamanca?
LEO.:   Es larga historia.
BAR.:   Un Bártulo seréis.
LEO.:   Ni aun un barbero.
Es, como digo, cosa muy notoria
en esta facultad lo que os refiero.
BAR.:   Sin duda que venís buen estudiante.
LEO.:   Saber he procurado lo importante.
BAR.:   Después que vemos tanto libro impreso,
no hay nadie que de sabio no presuma.
LEO.:   Antes, que ignoran más siento por eso,
por no se reducir a breve suma;
porque la confusión, con el exceso,
los intentos resuelve en vana espuma;
y aquel que de leer tiene más uso,
de ver letreros sólo está confuso.
No niego yo que de imprimir el arte
mil ingenios sacó de entre la jerga,
y que parece que en sagrada parte
sus obras guarda y contra el tiempo alberga:
este las destribuye y las reparte.
Débese esta invención a Gutenberga,

By my faith, *they're* the pumpkinheads!
    Then they tell us that a head of cattle[21] will die,
and later on it turns out to be in Transylvania;
that the vintage will be poor, whereas beer
will be more than plentiful in the German lands;
that the cherry crop will freeze in Gascony,
and that there will be a lot of tigers in Hyrcania.[22]
Finally, whether we plant crops or not,
the year still ends in December.

Enter the lawyer LEONELO *with* BARRILDO.

LEO.:   Believe me, you won't be the first to arrive,[23]
           because the "gossip corner" of the town square is already occupied.
BAR.:   How were things at Salamanca University?
LEO.:   That's a long story.
BAR.:   You'll be a Bartolo.[24]
LEO.:   Not even a barber.
           As I was saying, the matter I've been mentioning
           is very well known among lawyers.
BAR.:   I'm sure that you have returned as a fine scholar.
LEO.:   I've tried to learn what was most important.
BAR.:   Now that there are so many printed books,
           there's no one who doesn't set himself up as a learned man.
LEO.:   On the contrary: I think it's making people more ignorant,
           because information is no longer reduced to a handy compendium;
           you see, there's such a glut of matter that confusion
           turns people's attempts to learn into empty foam;
           and the man who spends the most time reading
           is merely confused by seeing all that verbiage.
              I don't deny that the art of printing
           has revealed a thousand talents amid the coarse cloth;[25]
           and that, as it seems, it preserves literary works
           as if in a sanctuary, protecting them from the ravages of time:
           it distributes them and shares them with others.
           This invention is due to Gutenberg,

---

21. Or: "an important personage."   22. Greco-Roman name of a Persian region
noted for its wild fauna.   23. Literally: "you won't win the cane." The first boy to arrive at school had the privilege of caning his fellow pupils when their teacher ordered
punishment.   24. This refers to the great fourteenth-century Italian jurist Bartolo di
Sassoferrato, the "Blackstone" of his day.   25. Or: "amid the jargon [or: 'gibberish']."

un famoso tudesco de Maguncia,
en quien la fama su valor renuncia.
      Mas muchos, que opinión tuvieron grave,
por imprimir sus obras la perdieron;
tras esto, con el nombre del que sabe,
muchos sus ignorancias imprimieron.
Otros, en quien la baja envidia cabe,
sus locos desatinos escribieron,
y con nombre de aquel que aborrecían,
impresos por el mundo los envían.

BAR.:   No soy de esa opinión.
LEO.:   El ignorante
es justo que se vengue del letrado.
BAR.:   Leonelo, la impresión es importante.
LEO.:   Sin ella muchos siglos se han pasado,
y no vemos que en este se levante
un Jerónimo santo, un Agustino.
BAR.:   Dejadlo y asentaos, que estáis mohíno.

Sale JUAN ROJO, *y otro* LABRADOR.

JUAN: No hay en cuatro haciendas para un dote,
si es que las vistas han de ser al uso;

que el hombre que es curioso es bien que note
que en esto el barrio y vulgo anda confuso.
LAB.:   ¿Qué hay del comendador? No os alborote.
JUAN: ¡Cuál a Laurencia en ese campo puso!
LAB.:   ¿Quién fue cual él tan bárbaro y lascivo?
Colgado le vea yo de aquel olivo.

Salen el COMENDADOR, ORTUÑO *y* FLORES.

COM.:   Dios guarde la buena gente.
REG.:   ¡Oh, señor!
COM.:   ¡Por vida mía,
que se estén!
ALO.:   Vusiñoría,

a celebrated German from Mainz,
thanks to whom Fame is giving up her old monopoly.
    But many writers who used to have a reputation for gravity
have lost it now that their works are in print;
moreover, falsely using the names of people who really know,
many ignorant writers have published their folly.
Others, filled with base envy,
have written their mad stupidities
and sent them off, printed, into the world
under the names of people they detest.

BAR.:   I don't feel as strongly as you do.

LEO.:   It's natural
for ignoramuses to take revenge on literate people.

BAR.:   Leonelo, printing *is* significant.

LEO.:   Many centuries have gone by without it,
and in our present age we don't see
a Saint Jerome or Augustine showing up.

BAR.:   Let it drop, and sit down, because you're cross.

Enter JUAN ROJO *and a* PEASANT.

JUAN: In four households there won't be enough for one dowry,
if the present custom of gifts between betrothed couples is to be
        kept up;
an alert, inquisitive man ought to observe
that, in this matter, the common folk and local people are confused.

PEA.:   What's new with the Commander? Don't get upset!

JUAN: The state he got Laurencia into!

PEA.:   Who was ever as barbarous and lustful as he is?
I'd like to see him swinging from that olive tree

Enter the COMMANDER, ORTUÑO, *and* FLORES.

COM.:   God keep all you good people.

COU.:   Oh, my lord!

COM.:   By my life,
let them remain seated!

ALO.:[26]   Your Lordship,

---

26. The lines marked "ALO[NSO]" in this edition are marked "ALCALDE" in standard
Spanish editions. Alonso and Esteban are joint mayors, and Esteban's lines are always
clearly marked with his own name. Hence the ascription here to Alonso, even though
he hasn't been mentioned in a stage direction.

adonde suele se siente,
    que en pie estaremos muy bien.
COM.:   Digo que se han de sentar.
EST.:   De los buenos es honrar,
    que no es posible que den
        honra los que no la tienen.
COM.:   Siéntense; hablaremos algo.
EST.:   ¿Vio vusiñoría el galgo?
COM.:   Alcalde, espantados vienen
    esos criados de ver
    tan notable ligereza.
EST.:   Es una extremada pieza.
    Pardiez, que puede correr
        a un lado de un delincuente
    o de un cobarde en quistión.
COM.:   Quisiera en esta ocasión
    que le hiciérades pariente
        a una liebre que por pies
    por momentos se me va.
EST.:   Sí haré, par Dios. ¿Dónde está?
COM.:   Allá: vuestra hija es.
EST.:   ¡Mi hija!
COM.:   Sí.
EST.:   Pues ¿es buena
    para alcanzada de vos?
COM.:   Reñilda, alcalde, por Dios.
EST.:   ¿Cómo?
COM.:   Ha dado en darme pena.
        Mujer hay, y principal,
    de alguno que está en la plaza,
    que dio, a la primera traza,
    traza de verme.
EST.:   Hizo mal;
        y vos, señor, no andáis bien
    en hablar tan libremente.
COM.:   ¡Oh, qué villano elocuente!
    ¡Ah, Flores!, haz que le den
        la *Política,* en que lea,
    de Aristóteles.
EST.:   Señor,
    debajo de vuestro honor
    vivir el pueblo desea.

please take your accustomed seat,
    because we'll be fine standing up.
COM.: I say that they are to sit down.
EST.: It is for good people to show honor,
because it isn't possible for those
    to give honor who don't possess it.
COM.: Let them sit down; we'll have a little chat.
EST.: Has your lordship seen the greyhound?
COM.: Mayor, these servants of mine
    were amazed to see
such exceptional speed.
EST.: It's an excellent animal.
I assure you, he can
    overtake a criminal
or a coward that the law is after.
COM.: On this occasion I'd like you
to match him against
    a hare that is continually
running away from me.
EST.: By God, I will! Where is it?
COM.: Over yonder: it's your daughter.
EST.:   My daughter!
COM.:   Yes.
EST.:   Then, is it right
for you to overtake her?
COM.: For God's sake, Mayor, give her a talking to!
EST.: What!?
COM.:   Her mind is set on grieving me.
    There's a woman, and one of the nobility,
the wife of someone who's here in the town square,
who, at the first hint of my intentions,
contrived a way to give me a tryst.
EST.:   She was wrong to do so;
    and you, my lord, are acting improperly
by speaking so licentiously.
COM.: Oh, what an eloquent peasant!
Ah, Flores, have him given
    a copy of Aristotle's *Politics*
to study.
EST.:   My lord,
the town wishes to live
under the protection of your honor.

       Mirad que en Fuenteovejuna
       hay gente muy principal.

LEO.:   ¿Viose desvergüenza igual?

COM.:   Pues ¿he dicho cosa alguna
       de que os pese, regidor?

REG.:   Lo que decís es injusto;
       no lo digáis, que no es justo
       que nos quitéis el honor.

COM.:   ¿Vosotros honor tenéis?
       ¡Qué freiles de Calatrava!

REG.:   Alguno acaso se alaba
       de la cruz que le ponéis,
         que no es de sangre tan limpia.

COM.:   ¿Y ensúciola yo, juntando
       la mía a la vuestra?

REG.:   Cuando
       que el mal más tiñe que alimpia.

COM.:   De cualquier suerte que sea,
       vuestras mujeres se honran.

ALO.:   Esas palabras les honran;
       las obras . . . no hay quien las crea.

COM.:   ¡Qué cansado villanaje!
       ¡Ah! Bien hayan las ciudades,
       que a hombres de calidades
       no hay quien sus gustos ataje;
         allá se precian casados
       que visiten sus mujeres.

EST.:   No harán; que con esto quieres
       que vivamos descuidados.
         En las ciudades hay Dios,
       y más presto quien castiga.

COM.:   ¡Levantaos de aquí!

ALO.:   ¡Que diga
       lo que escucháis por los dos!

COM.:   ¡Salí de la plaza luego!
       No quede ninguno aquí.

EST.:   Ya nos vamos.

	Please note that in Fuenteovejuna
	there are some highly illustrious people.
LEO.:	Was such shamelessness ever seen?
COM.:	Well, have I said anything
	to cause you discomfort, Councilman?
COU.:	What you're saying is unjust;
	don't say it, because it isn't just
	for you to deprive us of our honor.
COM.:	People like you have honor?
	A bunch of Knights of Calatrava!
COU.:	There may be some who boast
	about the Cross you sew on their robes
	who aren't of blood as pure as ours.
COM.:	And am I sullying it, when I associate
	my blood with yours?
COU.:	Yes, because
	evil ways stain rather than cleanse.
COM.:	No matter what my blood is like,
	I'm paying your wives an honor.
ALO.:	Those words are honorable;[27]
	as for the deeds—they're unbelievable.
COM.:	What a wearisome set of peasants!
	Ah, God bless big cities,
	where men of quality
	don't have their pleasures curtailed;
	there, husbands boast
	about their wives receiving visits.
EST.:	No, they don't; by saying that, you're trying
	to lull us into false security.
	Even in big cities God is present
	and an avenger is more ready to hand.
COM.:	Get out of here!
ALO.:	Consider the words
	you've heard him say as coming from both of us!
COM.:	Leave the square at once!
	Let no one remain here!
EST.:	We're going.

---

27. Many Spanish editors emend the line to *Esas palabras deshonran* ("Those words insult their honor").

COM.:   Pues no ansí.

FLO.:   Que te reportes te ruego.

COM.:   ¡Querrían hacer corrillo
los villanos en mi ausencia!

ORT.:   Ten un poco de paciencia.

COM.:   De tanta me maravillo.
            Cada uno de por sí
se vayan hasta sus casas.

LEO.:   ¡Cielo! ¿Que por esto pasas?

EST.:   Ya yo me voy por aquí.

Vanse.

COM.:   ¿Qué os parece de esta gente?

ORT.:   No sabes disimular
que no quieres escuchar
el disgusto que se siente.

COM.:   Estos ¿se igualan conmigo?

FLO.:   Que no es aqueso igualarse.

COM.:   Y el villano ¿ha de quedarse
con ballesta y sin castigo?

FLO.:   Anoche pensé que estaba
a la puerta de Laurencia,
y a otro, que su presencia
y su capilla imitaba,
            de oreja a oreja le di
un beneficio famoso.

COM.:   ¿Dónde estará aquel Frondoso?

FLO.:   Dicen que anda por ahí.

COM.:   ¿Por ahí se atreve a andar
hombre que matarme quiso?

FLO.:   Como el ave sin aviso,
o como el pez, viene a dar
al reclamo o al anzuelo.

COM.:   ¡Que a un capitán, cuya espada
tiemblan Córdoba y Granada,
un labrador, un mozuelo
            ponga una ballesta al pecho!
El mundo se acaba, Flores.

FLO.:   Como eso pueden amores.
Y pues que vives, sospecho

COM.:	But not like that!
FLO.:	Calm down, I beg you!
COM.:	These peasants want to form
	a secret gathering in my absence!
ORT.:	Have a little patience!
COM.:	I'm amazed I have so much.
	Let every one return
	home individually!
LEO.:	Heaven, you allow this to happen?
EST.:	I'm now leaving in this direction.

Exit [all except the COMMANDER *and his servants.]*

COM.:	What do you think about these people?
ORT.:	You don't know how to hide your feelings,
	because you refuse to hear
	how irritated they are.
COM.:	Are they trying to put themselves on my level?
FLO.:	That's not what they're trying to do.
COM.:	And that peasant, is he to remain
	in possession of my crossbow, and unpunished?
FLO.:	Last night I thought he was standing
	by Laurencia's door,
	and I did another man, who resembled him
	and was wearing the same short cloak,
	a tremendous "favor,"
	slashing him from ear to ear.
COM.:	Where can that Frondoso be?
FLO.:	They say he's in these parts.
COM ·	A man who tried to kill me
	has the nerve to remain around here?
FLO.:	Like a thoughtless bird,
	or a fish, he'll be lured
	by the whistle or end up hooked.
COM.:	That a general before whose sword
	Córdoba and Granada tremble,
	should have a peasant, a youngster,
	put a crossbow to his breast!
	The world is coming to an end, Flores.
FLO.:	That's what love can do.
	And, since you're still alive, I imagine

	que grande amistad le debes.
COM.:	Yo he disimulado, Ortuño;
	que si no, de punta a puño,
	antes de dos horas breves,
	pasara todo el lugar;
	que hasta que llegue ocasión
	al freno de la razón
	hago la venganza estar.
	¿Qué hay de Pascuala?
FLO.:	Responde
	que anda agora por casarse.
COM.:	¿Hasta allá quiere fiarse?
FLO.:	En fin, te remite donde
	te pagarán de contado.
COM.:	¿Qué hay de Olalla?
ORT.:	Una graciosa
	respuesta.
COM.:	Es moza briosa.
	¿Cómo?
ORT.:	Que su desposado
	anda tras ella estos días
	celoso de mis recados,
	y de que con tus crïados
	a visitalla venías;
	pero que si se descuida,
	entrarás como primero.
COM.:	¡Bueno, a fe de caballero!
	Pero el villanejo cuida . . .
ORT.:	Cuida, y anda por los aires.
COM.:	¿Qué hay de Inés?
FLO.:	¿Cuál?
COM.:	La de Antón.
FLO.:	Para cualquier ocasión
	te ha ofrecido sus donaires.
	Habléla por el corral,
	por donde has de entrar si quieres.
COM.:	A las fáciles mujeres
	quiero bien y pago mal.
	Si estas supiesen, oh Flores,
	estimarse en lo que valen . . .
FLO.:	No hay disgustos que se igualen

	you should be very grateful to him.
COM.:	I've concealed my feelings, Ortuño;
	otherwise, before two short hours had gone by
	I would have plunged my sword to the hilt
	into the whole town;
	as it is, until the right moment arrives,
	I'm forcing my revenge to be
	bridled by reason.
	What's new with Pascuala?
FLO.:	Her reply is
	that she's now about to be married.
COM.:	And she wants to live on credit up till then?
FLO.:	In short, she's directing you elsewhere,
	to a place where you'll be paid in cash.
COM.:	What about Olalla?
ORT.:	A witty
	reply.
COM.:	She's a high-spirited girl.
	What does she say?
ORT.:	That she's just been married, and her husband
	is keeping close tabs on her these days
	because my messages have made him jealous
	and because you were coming to visit her
	along with your servants;
	but, if he lets his guard down,
	you will be the first one in.
COM.:	Good, by the faith of a knight!
	But that little peasant is on the alert . . .
ORT.:	On the alert, and on his guard.
COM.:	What about Inés?
FLO.:	Which one?
COM.:	Antón's wife.
FLO.:	She has offered you her charms
	for any time you're ready.
	I spoke to her across the yard,
	through which you can go in if you like.
COM.:	Easy women
	I like well but reward badly.
	Oh, Flores, if they only knew how to
	rate themselves at their true worth . . .
FLO.:	There's nothing so vexing

a contrastar sus favores.
   Rendirse presto desdice
de la esperanza del bien;
mas hay mujeres también,
por que el filósofo dice,
   que apetecen a los hombres
como la forma desea
la materia; y que esto sea
así, no hay de que te asombres.

COM.:   Un hombre de amores loco
huélgase que a su accidente
se le rindan fácilmente,
mas después las tiene en poco,
   y el camino de olvidar,
al hombre más obligado,
es haber poco costado
lo que pudo desear.

Sale CIMBRANOS, *soldado.*

CIM.:   ¿Está aquí el comendador?
ORT.:   ¿No le ves en tu presencia?
CIM.:   ¡Oh, gallardo Fernán Gómez!
Trueca la verde montera
en el blanco morrïón,
y el gabán en armas nuevas,
que el maestre de Santiago
y el conde de Cabra cercan
a don Rodrigo Girón,
por la castellana reina,
en Ciudad Real; de suerte
que no es mucho que se pierda
lo que en Calatrava sabes
que tanta sangre le cuesta.
Ya divisan con las luces,
desde las altas almenas,
los castillos y leones
y barras aragonesas.
Y aunque el rey de Portugal
honrar a Girón quisiera,
no hará poco en que el maestre

as to win their favors.
   A quick surrender cuts short
a man's hopes for satisfaction;
but there are also women
about whom Aristotle says
   that they crave for men
just as form longs for
matter; and you shouldn't be surprised
that such is the case.

COM.:   A man crazed by love
is pleased when they give in
easily to his passion,
but afterwards he scorns them,
   and, even for a man they have most greatly obliged,
the road to forgetting them
is having paid too little
for what he happened to desire.

Enter CIMBRANOS, *a soldier.*

CIM.:   Is the Commander here?
ORT.:   Don't you see him right before you?
CIM.:   Oh, valiant Fernán Gómez!
Exchange your green hunting cap
for a gleaming helmet,
and your robe for new armor,
because the Master of Santiago
and the Count of Cabra are besieging
Don Rodrigo Girón,
on behalf of the Queen of Castile,
in Ciudad Real; so that
it won't take long to lose
all that it cost so much
Calatrava blood to win, as you know.
Now at daylight they can make out,
from the lofty battlements,
the castles of Castile, the lions of León,
and the heraldic bars of Aragon on their banners.
And, even though the king of Portugal
would like to honor Girón,
it will be no small thing if the Master

a Almagro con vida vuelva.
Ponte a caballo, señor,
que sólo con que te vean,
se volverán a Castilla.
COM.:   No prosigas; tente, espera.
Haz, Ortuño, que en la plaza
toquen luego una trompeta.
¿Qué soldados tengo aquí?
ORT.:   Pienso que tienes cincuenta.
COM.:   Pónganse a caballo todos.
CIM.:   Si no caminas apriesa,
Ciudad Real es del rey.
COM.:   No hayas miedo que lo sea.

Vanse.
Salen MENGO *y* LAURENCIA *y* PASCUALA, *huyendo.*

PAS.:   No te apartes de nosotras.
MEN.:   Pues ¿aquí tenéis temor?
LAU.:   Mengo, a la villa es mejor
que vamos unas con otras,
        pues que no hay hombre ninguno,
por que no demos con él.
MEN.:   ¡Que este demonio crüel
nos sea tan importuno!
LAU.:   No nos deja a sol ni a sombra.
MEN.:   ¡Oh, rayo del cielo baje
que sus locuras ataje!
LAU.:   Sangrienta fiera le nombra,
        arsénico y pestilencia
del lugar.
MEN.:   Hanme contado
que Frondoso, aquí en el prado,
para librarte, Laurencia,
        le puso al pecho una jara.
LAU.:   Los hombres aborrecía,
Mengo, mas desde aquel día
los miro con otra cara.
        ¡Gran valor tuvo Frondoso!
Pienso que le ha de costar
la vida.

gets back to Almagro alive.
Mount your horse, my lord,
because at the mere sight of you,
the enemy will return to Castile.

COM.:   Don't go on; restrain yourself, wait.
Ortuño, let a trumpet be sounded
in the square immediately.
What soldiers do I have here?

ORT.:   I think you have fifty.

COM.:   Let them all mount.

CIM.:   If you don't set out quickly,
Ciudad Real will fall to the King.

COM.:   Have no fear of such an event.

Exit.
Enter MENGO, LAURENCIA, *and* PASCUALA, *on the run.*

PAS.:   Mengo, don't leave us alone.

MEN.:   What? You're afraid here?

LAU.:   Mengo, it's better for us women to go
to town in a group,
    seeing there are no men around,
in case we run across *him.*

MEN.:   That this cruel devil
should molest us so!

LAU.:   He doesn't let us alone in sunshine or in shade.

MEN.:   Oh, may a thunderbolt descend from heaven
and put an end to his mad ways!

LAU.:   Rather, call him a bloodthirsty beast,
    the arsenic and plague
of the town.

MEN.:   I've been told
that Frondoso, here in the meadow,
to save you, Laurencia,
    put an arrow to his breast.

LAU.:   I used to hate men,
Mengo, but ever since that day
I've been viewing them with other eyes.
    Frondoso was really brave!
I'm afraid it will cost him
his life.

MEN.:   Que del lugar
se vaya, será forzoso.

LAU.:   Aunque ya le quiero bien,
eso mismo le aconsejo;
mas recibe mi consejo
con ira, rabia y desdén;
y jura el comendador
que le ha de colgar de un pie.

PAS.:   ¡Mal garrotillo le dé!

MEN.:   Mala pedrada es mejor.
¡Voto al sol, si le tirara
con la que llevo al apero,
que al sonar el crujidero,
al casco se la encajara!
No fue Sábalo, el romano,
tan vicioso por jamás.

LAU.:   Heliogábalo dirás,
más que una fiera inhumano.

MEN.:   Pero Galván, o quien fue,
que yo no entiendo de historia,
mas su cativa memoria
vencida de este se ve.
¿Hay hombre en naturaleza
como Fernán Gómez?

PAS.:   No;
que parece que le dio
de una tigre la aspereza.

Sale JACINTA.

JAC.:   Dadme socorro, por Dios,
si la amistad os obliga.

LAU.:   ¿Qué es esto, Jacinta, amiga?

PAS.:   Tuyas lo somos las dos.

JAC.:   Del comendador crïados,
que van a Ciudad Real,
más de infamia natural
que de noble acero armados,
me quieren llevar a él.

MEN.:   It will be necessary
         for him to leave town.

LAU.:   Even though I'm now fond of him,
         I've been giving him the same advice;
         but he receives my advice
         with anger, rage, and scorn;
                  and the Commander has sworn an oath
         to hang him up by the feet.

PAS.:   I hope he gets diphtheria!

MEN.:   A real stoning would be better.
                  I swear to God that, if I took a shot at him
         with the sling I wear when out working in the fields,
         at the creaking of the straps
         I'd drive the stone into his skull!
                  Even the Roman emperor Sábalo[28]
         was never that lustful.

LAU.:   You mean Heliogabalus,
         who was more inhuman than a wild animal.

MEN.:   Even Galván,[29] or whoever it was,
         because I don't know much about history,
         has his bad reputation
         surpassed by this fellow.
                  Does Nature contain
         another man like Fernán Gómez?

PAS.:   No;
         he seems to have acquired
         his ruggedness from a tiger.

Enter JACINTA.

JAC.:   Help me for the love of God,
         if you feel bound by friendship!

LAU.:   What's wrong, my friend Jacinta?

PAS.:   Both of us women are at your service.

JAC.:   Servants of the Commander,
         on their way to Ciudad Real,
         armed more with natural infamy
         than with noble steel,
                  want to carry me off to him.

---

28. Mengo's corruption of the emperor's name actually means "shad" in Spanish.
29. An evil character in old narrative ballads.

LAU.:   Pues, Jacinta, Dios te libre,
que cuando contigo es libre,
conmigo será crüel.

Vase.

PAS.:   Jacinta, yo no soy hombre
que te puedo defender.

Vase.

MEN.:   Yo sí lo tengo de ser,
porque tengo el ser y el nombre.   *obligación/*
Llégate, Jacinta, a mí.   *honor*
JAC.:   ¿Tienes armas?
MEN.:   Las primeras
del mundo.
JAC.:   ¡Oh, si las tuvieras!
MEN.:   Piedras hay, Jacinta, aquí.

Salen FLORES *y* ORTUÑO.

FLO.:   ¿Por los pies pensabas irte?
JAC.:   Mengo, ¡muerta soy!
MEN.:   Señores . . .
¿A estos pobres labradores? . . .
ORT.:   Pues ¿tú quieres persuadirte
a defender la mujer?
MEN.:   Con los ruegos la defiendo;
que soy su deudo y pretendo
guardalla, si puede ser.
FLO.:   Quitalde luego la vida.
MEN.:   ¡Voto al sol, si me emberrincho
y el cáñamo me descincho,
que la llevéis bien vendida!

Salen el COMENDADOR *y* CIMBRANOS.

COM.:   ¿Qué es eso? ¿A cosas tan viles
me habéis de hacer apear?
FLO.:   Gente de este vil lugar

LAU.:   Well, Jacinta, may God save you!
            Because, if he is licentious to you,
            he'll be cruel to me.

She exits.

PAS.:   Jacinta, I'm not a man
           and I can't protect you.

She exits.

MEN.:   Well, I do have to be a man,
           since I have the form and the name of one.

[handwritten: What kind of man would he be if he left ??]

           Come over to me, Jacinta.
JAC.:   Do you have any weapons?
MEN.:   The first ones
           ever invented.
JAC.:   Oh, if you only had some!
MEN.:   There are stones right here, Jacinta.

Enter FLORES and ORTUÑO.

FLO.:   You thought you could run away?
JAC.:   Mengo, I'm as good as dead!
MEN.:   Gentlemen . . .
           You're after such poor peasants? . . .
ORT.:   So, you're trying to work up the courage
           to protect this woman?
MEN.:   I'm protecting her with entreaties;
           because I'm a relative of hers, and I mean
           to defend her if possible.
FLO.:   Kill him at once!
MEN.:   By God, if I get worked up
           and take the sling out of my belt,
           you've got something coming to you!

Enter the COMMANDER and CIMBRANOS.

COM.:   What's all this? For such base matters
           you have to make me dismount?
FLO.:   The people in this base town

(que ya es razón que aniquiles,
  pues en nada te da gusto)
a nuestras armas se atreve.
MEN.:   Señor, si piedad os mueve
de soceso tan injusto,
  castigad estos soldados,
que con vuestro nombre agora
roban una labradora
a esposo y padres honrados;
  y dadme licencia a mí
que se la pueda llevar.
COM.:   Licencia les quiero dar . . .
para vengarse de ti.
  Suelta la honda.
MEN.:   ¡Señor! . . .
COM.:   Flores, Ortuño, Cimbranos,
con ella le atad las manos.
MEN.:   ¿Así volvéis por su honor?
COM.:   ¿Qué piensan Fuenteovejuna
y sus villanos de mí?
MEN.:   Señor, ¿en qué os ofendí,
ni el pueblo en cosa ninguna?
FLO.:   ¿Ha de morir?
COM.:   No ensuciéis
las armas que habéis de honrar
en otro mejor lugar.
ORT.:   ¿Qué mandas?
COM.:   Que lo azotéis.
  Llevalde, y en ese roble
le atad y le desnudad,
y con las riendas . . .
MEN.:   ¡Piedad!
¡Piedad, pues sois hombre noble!
COM.:   . . . azotalde hasta que salten
los hierros de las correas.
MEN.:   ¡Cielos! ¿A hazañas tan feas
queréis que castigos falten?

Vanse.

COM.:   Tú, villana, ¿por qué huyes?
¿Es mejor un labrador

(which by now it's right for you to destroy,
    because it gives you no pleasure in any way)
are emboldened to confront our weaponry.

MEN.:   My lord, if you are moved to pity
    by such an unjust occurrence,
        punish these soldiers,
    who now, under cover of your name,
    are abducting a peasant woman
    from her respectable husband and parents;
        and give me permission
    to take her away with me.

COM.:   I give *them* permission
    to take revenge on *you*.
        Drop that sling!

MEN.:   My lord! . . .

COM.:   Flores, Ortuño, Cimbranos,
    tie his hands with it.

MEN.:   Is this how you look to her honor?

COM.:   What do Fuenteovejuna
    and its peasants think of me?

MEN.:   My lord, how have I offended you,
    I or the town, in any way?

FLO.:   Is he to die?

COM.:   Don't sully
    the weapons that you must honor
    in another, better place.

ORT.:   What are your orders?

COM.:   That you whip him.
    Take him, tie him
    to that oak, stripped,
    and with the reins . . .

MEN.:   Mercy!
    Mercy, since you're a nobleman!

COM.:   . . . whip him until the metal parts
    pop off the leather straps.

MEN.:   Heavens! Do you send
    no punishment for such ugly deeds?

Exit [all except the COMMANDER, *some retinue, and* JACINTA].

COM.:   And you, peasant woman, why are you running away?
    Is a plowman preferable

JAC.:   que un hombre de mi valor?
JAC.:   ¡Harto bien me restituyes
      el honor que me han quitado
    en llevarme para ti!
COM.:   ¿En quererte llevar?
JAC.:   Sí:
    porque tengo un padre honrado,
      que si en alto nacimiento
    no te iguala, en las costumbres
    te vence.
COM.:   Las pesadumbres
    y el villano atrevimiento
      no tiemplan bien un airado.
    Tira por ahí.
JAC.:   ¿Con quién?
COM.:   Conmigo.
JAC.:   Míralo bien.
COM.:   Para tu mal lo he mirado.
      Ya no mía, del bagaje
    del ejército has de ser.
JAC.:   No tiene el mundo poder
    para hacerme, viva, ultraje.
COM.:   Ea, villana, camina.
JAC.:   ¡Piedad, señor!
COM.:   No hay piedad.
JAC.:   Apelo de tu crueldad
    a la justicia divina.

Llévanla y vanse, y salen LAURENCIA *y* FRONDOSO.

LAU.:   ¿Cómo así a venir te atreves,
    sin temer tu daño?
FRO.:   Ha sido
    dar testimonio cumplido
    de la afición que me debes.
      Desde aquel recuesto vi
    salir al comendador,
    y fiado en tu valor,
    todo mi temor perdí.
      Vaya donde no le vean
    volver.

	to a man of my worth?
JAC.:	It's a fine way that you're restoring
	the honor they deprived me of
	by abducting me for you!
COM.:	By trying to abduct you?
JAC.:	Yes:
	because I have a respectable father,
	who, if he isn't your equal
	in high birth, surpasses you
	in his way of life.
COM.:	Grieving a man,
	and brazenly flouting him like a peasant,
	doesn't calm him down when he's angry.
	Move over here!
JAC.:	With whom?
COM.:	With me.
JAC.:	Heed what you're doing.
COM.:	I've heeded it, to your misfortune.
	I no longer want you for myself; you'll be
	part of the army's supplies.
JAC.:	The world has no power
	to violate me while I'm alive.
COM.:	Go on, peasant, walk!
JAC.:	Mercy, my lord!
COM.:	I have no mercy.
JAC.:	I call your cruelty to the attention
	of divine justice.

They take her away and exit. Enter LAURENCIA *and* FRONDOSO.

LAU.:	How are you bold enough to come here this way
	without fearing harm to yourself?
FRO.:	It was
	to prove to you completely
	how much you ought to care for me.
	From that hillside I saw
	the Commander leaving,
	and, trusting in your worth,
	I lost all my fear.
	May he go to a place from which he'll never be seen
	returning.

LAU.:   Tente en maldecir,
porque suele más vivir
al que la muerte desean.

FRO.:   Si es eso, viva mil años,
y así se hará todo bien,
pues deseándole bien
estarán ciertos sus daños.
Laurencia, deseo saber
si vive en ti mi cuidado,
y si mi lealtad ha hallado
el puerto de merecer.
Mira que toda la villa
ya para en uno nos tiene;
y de cómo a ser no viene,
la villa se maravilla.
Los desdeñosos extremos
deja, y responde no o sí.

LAU.: Pues a la villa y a ti
respondo que lo seremos.

FRO.:   Deja que tus plantas bese
por la merced recebida,
pues el cobrar nueva vida
por ella es bien que confiese.

LAU.: De cumplimientos acorta;
y para que mejor cuadre,
habla, Frondoso, a mi padre,
pues es lo que más importa,
  que allí viene con mi tío;
y fía que ha de tener
ser, Frondoso, tu mujer,
buen suceso.

FRO.:   En Dios confío.

Escóndese.

Salen ESTEBAN, ALONSO, *y* JUAN ROJO.

ALO.:   Fue su término de modo,
que la plaza alborotó:

LAU.:   Stop cursing him,
because generally a person
whom people wish dead lives all the longer.

FRO.:   If that's the case, may he live a thousand years,
and, that way, everything will turn out well,
because, when I wish him well,
he'll be sure to suffer for it.
          Laurencia, I want to know
whether you have any concern for my well-being,
and whether my faithfulness has found
the haven of being worthy of you.
          Look: the whole town
already considers us a couple;
and the town is amazed
that it doesn't actually happen.
          Leave off the extremity
of your disdain, and answer yes or no.

LAU.:   Well, then, to the town and to you
I reply that we *will* be one.

FLO.:   Let me kiss your feet
for the favor I have received,
since it's only right for me to confess
that it has given me a new lease on life.

LAU.:   Cut short your polite remarks;
and, in order that the whole thing is done properly,
speak to my father, Frondoso,
since that's the most important matter;
          he's coming this way with my uncle;
and, Frondoso, be confident
that my being your wife
will come to pass.

FRO.:   I trust in God.

He hides.
Enter ESTEBAN, ALONSO, *and* JUAN ROJO.[30]

ALO.:   It ended up in such a way
that he threw the whole square into confusion:

---

30. In standard Spanish editions, Alonso is here called the Mayor, and Juan Rojo is called the Councilman. See footnotes 20 and 26 for an explanation of the wording in this edition.

en efeto, procedió
muy descomedido en todo.
    No hay a quien admiración
sus demasías no den;
la pobre Jacinta es quien
pierde por su sinrazón.

JUAN: Ya a los Católicos Reyes,
que este nombre les dan ya,
presto España les dará
la obediencia de sus leyes.
    Ya sobre Ciudad Real,
contra el Girón que la tiene,
Santiago a caballo viene
por capitán general.
    Pésame; que era Jacinta
doncella de buena pro.

ALO.:   Luego, ¿a Mengo le azotó?

JUAN: No hay negra bayeta o tinta
como sus carnes están.

ALO.:   Callad; que me siento arder,
viendo su mal proceder,
y el mal nombre que le dan.
    Yo ¿para qué traigo aquí
este palo sin provecho?

JUAN: Si sus crïados lo han hecho,
¿de qué os afligís ansí?

ALO.:   ¿Queréis más? Que me contaron
que a la de Pedro Redondo
un día, que en lo más hondo
de este valle la encontraron,
    después de sus insolencias,
a sus crïados la dio.

JUAN: Aquí hay gente. ¿Quién es?

FRO.:   Yo,
que espero vuestras licencias.

JUAN: Para mi casa, Frondoso,
licencia no es menester;
debes a tu padre el ser,
y a mí otro ser amoroso.

	in fact, his procedure
	was very immoderate in every way.
	There's no one who isn't amazed
	by his excesses;
	poor Jacinta is the loser
	by his madness.
JUAN:	Now Spain will soon give
	the Catholic Monarchs,
	who are already known by that name,
	her legal allegiance.
	Already Santiago is riding
	as general
	toward Ciudad Real
	against Girón, who is holding it.
	I'm sorry, because Jacinta
	was a decent young woman.
ALO.:	Then, he whipped Mengo?
JUAN:	There's no black flannel or ink
	as dark as his flesh.
ALO.:	Be silent, because I feel as if I were on fire,
	seeing his improper ways
	and the bad name people give him.
	As for me, to what purpose am I here carrying
	this useless piece of wood?[31]
JUAN:	If it was his servants who did it,
	why are you so upset?
ALO.:	You want more? Well, I've been told
	that, one day, when they came across
	Pedro Redondo's wife
	in the deepest part of this valley,
	after insulting her,
	he handed her over to his servants.
JUAN:	There's someone here. Who is it?
FRO.:	I,
	I'm awaiting your permission to speak.
JUAN:	In my house, Frondoso,
	you have no need of permission;
	you owe your existence to your father,
	and to me a second existence founded on love.

31. His mayoral staff of office.

    Hete criado, y te quiero
    como a hijo.
FRO.:   Pues, señor,
    fiado en aquese amor,
    de ti una merced espero.
    Ya sabes de quién soy hijo.
EST.:   ¿Hate agraviado ese loco
    de Fernán Gómez?
FRO.:   No poco.
EST.:   El corazón me lo dijo.
FRO.:   Pues, señor, con el seguro
    del amor que habéis mostrado,
    de Laurencia enamorado,
    el ser su esposo procuro.
    Perdona si en el pedir
    mi lengua se ha adelantado;
    que he sido en decirlo osado,
    como otro lo ha de decir.
EST.:   Vienes, Frondoso, a ocasión
    que me alargarás la vida,
    por la cosa más temida
    que siente mi corazón.
    Agradezco, hijo, al cielo
    que así vuelvas por mi honor,
    y agradézcole a tu amor
    la limpieza de tu celo.
    Mas, como es justo, es razón
    dar cuenta a tu padre de esto;
    sólo digo que estoy presto,
    en sabiendo su intención;
    que yo dichoso me hallo
    en que aqueso llegue a ser.
JUAN: De la moza el parecer
    tomad, antes de acetallo.
EST.:   No tengáis de eso cuidado,
    que ya el caso está dispuesto:
    antes de venir a esto,
    entre ellos se ha concertado.
    En el dote, si advertís,

It was I who raised you, and I love you
like a son.

FRO.:   Then, sir,
trusting in that love,
I await a favor from you.
    You already know whose son I am.

EST.:   Has that madman Fernán Gómez
affronted you?

FRO.:   Extremely.

EST.:   My heart told me so.

FRO.:   Well, then, sir, on the basis
of the love you two have shown me,
since I am in love with Laurencia,
I wish to become her husband.
    Pardon me if, in making this request,
my tongue has gone too fast,
and I've been too bold in stating it,
seeing that someone else[32] ought to make the request.

EST.:   Frondoso, your coming here with it
will increase my life span,
because you're ridding me of the greatest fear
that my heart feels.
    Son, I thank heaven
that you are returning this way to save my honor,
and I thank your love
for the purity of its passion.
    But, as is only proper, it's right
for you to inform your father of this;
I merely say that I am ready on my part,
as soon as I learn his wishes;
    because I consider myself fortunate
if this comes to pass.

JUAN: Get the girl's opinion
before you accept him.

EST.:   Have no concern about that,
because the matter is already settled:
before it got this far,
it was agreed upon between them.
    Concerning the dowry, if that's on your mind,

---

32. His father.

se puede agora tratar,
que por bien os pienso dar
algunos maravedís.

FRO.:   Yo dote no he menester,
de eso no hay que entristeceros.

JUAN: Pues que no la pide en cueros
lo podéis agradecer.

EST.:   Tomaré el parecer de ella
si os parece; será bien.

FRO.:   Justo es; que no hace bien
quien los gustos atropella.

EST.:   ¡Hija! ¡Laurencia! . . .

LAU.:   Señor . . .

EST.:   Mirad si digo bien yo.
¡Ved qué presto respondió!
Hija, Laurencia, mi amor
    a preguntarte ha venido
(apártate aquí) si es bien
que a Gila, tu amiga, den
a Frondoso por marido,
    que es un honrado zagal,
si le hay en Fuenteovejuna . . .

LAU.:   ¿Gila se casa?

EST.:   Y si alguna
le merece y es su igual . . .

LAU.:   Yo digo, señor, que sí.

EST.:   Sí; mas yo digo que es fea
y que harto mejor se emplea
Frondoso, Laurencia, en ti.

LAU.:   ¿Aún no se te han olvidado
los donaires con la edad?

EST.:   ¿Quiéresle tú?

LAU.:   Voluntad
le he tenido y le he cobrado;
    pero por lo que tú sabes . . .

EST.:   ¿Quieres tú que diga sí?

LAU.:   Dilo tú, señor, por mí.

EST.:   ¿Yo? ¿Pues tengo yo las llaves?
    Hecho está. Ven, buscaremos
a mi compadre en la plaza.

JUAN: Vamos.

we can negotiate now,
because I certainly intend to give you
some money.

FRO.:   I don't need a dowry,
so there's no cause to worry yourself about that.

JUAN: Well, you can be grateful
that he's not asking for her in the buff!

EST.:   I'll get her opinion
if you think I should; it's a good idea.

FRO.:   It's only fair; because it's wrong
to ride roughshod over people's feelings.

EST.:   Daughter! Laurencia! . . .

LAU.:   Sir . . .

EST.:   Just see whether I'm right or not!
Did you notice how quickly she replied?
Daughter, Laurencia, my fatherly love
    leads me to ask you—
step over here with me—whether it's all right
for your friend Gila to get
Frondoso for a husband;
    he's a respectable young man
if there is one in Fuenteovejuna . . .

LAU.:   Gila is getting married?

EST.:   And if any girl
deserves him and is a good match for him . . .

LAU.:   I give my approval, sir.

EST.:   Yes, but I say that she's ugly
and that Frondoso would be much better bestowed
on you, Laurencia.

LAU.,;   You still haven't given up
joking at your age?

EST.:   Do you love him?

LAU.:   I have felt
an inclination toward him, which he has requited,
    but, for the reasons that you know . . .

EST.:   Do you want me to give my consent?

LAU.:   Give it on my behalf, sir.

EST.:   I? Am I the one holding the keys?
    The matter is settled. Come, we'll look for
my neighbor in the square.

JUAN: Let's go.

EST.:	Hijo, y en la traza
	del dote, ¿qué le diremos?
	Que yo bien te puedo dar
	cuatro mil maravedís.
FRO.:	Señor, ¿eso me decís?
	Mi honor queréis agraviar.
EST.:	Anda, hijo, que eso es
	cosa que pasa en un día;
	que si no hay dote, a fe mía
	que se echa menos después.

Vanse, y queda FRONDOSO *y* LAURENCIA.

LAU.:	Di, Frondoso, ¿estás contento?
FRO.:	¡Cómo si lo estoy! ¡Es poco,
	pues que no me vuelvo loco
	de gozo del bien que siento!
	Risa vierte el corazón
	por los ojos, de alegría,
	viéndote, Laurencia mía,
	en tan dulce posesión.

Vanse.
Salen el MAESTRE, *el* COMENDADOR, FLORES *y* ORTUÑO.

COM.:	Huye, señor, que no hay otro remedio.
MAE.:	La flaqueza del muro lo ha causado,
	y el poderoso ejército enemigo.
COM.:	Sangre les cuesta y infinitas vidas.
MAE.:	Y no se alabarán que en sus despojos
	pondrán nuestro pendón de Calatrava,
	que a honrar su empresa y los demás bastaba.
COM.:	Tus desinios, Girón, quedan perdidos.
MAE.:	¿Qué puedo hacer, si la fortuna ciega
	a quien hoy levantó mañana humilla?
DENTRO:	¡Vitoria por los reyes de Castilla!
MAE.:	Ya coronan de luces las almenas,
	y las ventanas de las torres altas
	entoldan con pendones vitoriosos.
COM.:	Bien pudieran de sangre que les cuesta.
	A fe que es más tragedia que no fiesta.

[Anotaciones manuscritas en el margen: "escena política"; "españoles reconquista la ciudad"]

EST.:   Son, with regard to
              the dowry, what shall we tell him?
              Because I can easily give you
              four thousand *maravedís.*
FRO.:   Sir, are you saying that to me?
              You want to insult my honor.
EST.:   Come now, son, such feelings
              go by in a day;
              because, by my faith, when there's no dowry,
              it's sorely missed later on.

              Exit all except FRONDOSO *and* LAURENCIA.

LAU.:   Tell me, Frondoso, are you contented?
FRO.:   I'll say I am! It's a wonder
              that I don't go crazy
              with joy, I feel so good!
                  My heart sheds laughter
              through my eyes, from happiness,
              when I see you, my Laurencia,
              so sweetly in my possession.

                          Exit.
              Enter the MASTER, *the* COMMANDER, FLORES, *and* ORTUÑO.

COM.:   Flee, sir, for there's no other recourse!
MAS.:   The weakness of the city wall was responsible,
              as well as the might of the enemy's army.
COM.:   It costs them blood and innumerable lives.
MAS.:   Nor will they boast that among their spoils
              they will place our banner of Calatrava,
              which would have been enough to honor their heraldic device and
                  the other banners.
COM.:   Girón, your plans are destroyed.
MAS.:   What can I do if blind Fortune
              raises up a man one day only to humble him the next?
SHOUTS WITHIN: Victory for the King and Queen of Castile!
MAS.:   They are now crowning the battlements with lights
              and shading the windows of the high towers
              with pennants of victory.
COM.:   And so they might, for all the blood it cost them!
              By my faith, it's more of a tragedy than a celebration.

MAE.:   Yo vuelvo a Calatrava, Fernán Gómez.

COM.:   Y yo a Fuenteovejuna, mientras tratas
o seguir esta parte de tus deudos,
o reducir la tuya al Rey Católico.

MAE.:   Yo te diré por cartas lo que intento.

COM.:   El tiempo ha de enseñarte.

MAE.   ¡Ah, pocos años,
sujetos al rigor de sus engaños!

Sale la boda, MÚSICOS, MENGO, FRONDOSO, LAURENCIA, PASCUALA,
BARRILDO, ESTEBAN, ALONSO *y* JUAN ROJO.

MÚS.:   *¡Vivan muchos años*
los desposados!
¡Vivan muchos años!

MEN.:   A fe, que no os ha costado
mucho trabajo el cantar.

BAR.:   ¿Supiéraslo tú trovar
mejor que él está trovado?

FRO.:   Mejor entiende de azotes
Mengo, que de versos ya.

MEN.:   Alguno en el valle está,
para que no te alborotes,
a quien el comendador . . .

BAR.:   No lo digas, por tu vida;
que este bárbaro humicida
a todos quita el honor.

MEN.:   Que me azotasen a mí
cien soldados aquel día . . .
Sola una honda tenía;
harto desdichado fui.
Pero que le hayan echado
una melecina a un hombre,
que, aunque no diré su nombre,
todos saben que es honrado,
llena de tinta y de chinas,
¿cómo se puede sufrir?

BAR.:   Haríalo por reír.

MEN.:   No hay risa con melecinas;

MAS.:   I'm returning to Calatrava territory, Fernán Gómez.
COM.:   And I to Fuenteovejuna, while you decide
           whether to continue in the faction of your relatives
           or transfer your allegiance to the Catholic King.
MAS.:   I'll let you know my intentions by letter.
COM.:   Time will instruct you.
MAS.:   Ah, youth,
           subject to the severity of its mistakes!

Enter the wedding party, MUSICIANS, MENGO, FRONDOSO, LAURENCIA,
   PASCUALA, BARRILDO, ESTEBAN, ALONSO,[33] *and* JUAN ROJO.

MUS.:   "Long life
           to the newlyweds!
           Long life!"
MEN.:   By my faith, that song
           didn't cost you a great effort.
BAR.:   Would you be able to write
           better words than those?
FRO.:   Mengo now knows more
           about lashes than verses.
MEN.:   There's someone in the valley—
           don't let this upset you—
              whom the Commander . . .
BAR.:   On your life, don't say it;
           because that murderous barbarian
           deprives everyone of their honor.
MEN.:   To think that a hundred soldiers
           whipped me that day . . .
           I had only a sling;
           I was really unlucky.
              But that they gave
           an enema to a man
           who, though I won't mention his name,
           is known to one and all to be respectable—
              and an enema full of ink and pebbles—
           how can anyone stand for that?
BAR.:   He must have done it for a laugh.
MEN.:   Enemas are no laughing matter;

---

33. Called "the Mayor" in standard Spanish editions.

	que aunque es cosa saludable . . .
	yo me quiero morir luego.
Fro.:	Vaya la copla, te ruego,
	si es la copla razonable.

BAR.:   *Vivan muchos años juntos*
           los novios, ruego a los cielos,
           y por envidias ni celos
           ni riñan ni anden en puntos.
           Lleven a entrambos difuntos,
           de puro vivir cansados.
           ¡Vivan muchos años!

MEN.:   ¡Maldiga el cielo el poeta
           que tal coplón arrojó!

BAR.:   Fue muy presto . . .

MEN.:   Pienso yo
           una cosa de esta seta:
               ¿no habéis visto un buñolero,
           en el aceite abrasando
           pedazos de masa echando
           hasta llenarse el caldero?
               Que unos le salen hinchados,
           otros tuertos y mal hechos,
           ya zurdos y ya derechos,
           ya fritos y ya quemados.
               Pues así imagino yo
           un poeta componiendo,
           la materia previniendo,
           que es quien la masa le dio:
               va arrojando verso aprisa
           al caldero del papel,
           confiado en que la miel
           cubrirá la burla y risa.
               Mas poniéndolo en el pecho,
           apenas hay quien los tome,
           tanto que sólo los come
           el mismo que los ha hecho.

BAR.:   Déjate ya de locuras;
           deja los novios hablar.

LAU.:   Las manos nos da a besar.

JUAN: Hija, ¿mi mano procuras?
               Pídela a tu padre luego

	because, even though they may be good for your health . . .
	I prefer dying at once.
FRO.:	Let's hear the refrain, please,
	if it makes any sense.
BAR.:	"May the newlyweds live many years
	side by side, I beg heaven,
	and may neither envy nor jealousy
	make them quarrel or fight over trifles.
	May their dead bodies be carried out
	only after they're worn out with hearty living!
	Long life to them!"
MEN.:	May heaven curse the poet
	who dashed off a refrain like that one!
BAR.:	It was quickly improvised . . .
MEN.:	There's an idea

I have about the poetic crew:
   haven't you ever seen a fritter vendor
tossing pieces of dough
into the boiling oil
until the kettle is filled?
   Some of them turn out swollen,
others twisted and misshapen,
now longer on the left side, now longer on the right,
now fried and now burnt.
   Well, that's how I picture
a poet composing,
preparing his material,
which is what provided his dough:
   he keeps on quickly tossing verses
onto the paper (his kettle),
trusting that the honey coating
will cover up the mockery and laughter.
   But when he displays them to customers,
hardly anyone buys them,
so that the only one who eats them
is the man who made them.

BAR.:	Enough of your folly now;
	let the newlyweds speak.
LAU.:	Give us your hands to kiss.
JUAN:	My girl, you want my hand?
	First ask your father for his,

	para ti y para Frondoso.
EST.:	Rojo, a ella y a su esposo
	que se la dé el cielo ruego,
	con su larga bendición.
FRO.:	Los dos a los dos la echad.
JUAN:	Ea, tañed y cantad,
	pues que para en uno son.
MÚS.:	*Al val de Fuenteovejuna*

la niña en cabello baja;
el caballero la sigue
de la cruz de Calatrava.
Entre las ramas se esconde,
de vergonzosa y turbada;
fingiendo que no le ha visto,
pone delante las ramas.
«¿Para qué te ascondes,
niña gallarda?
Que mis linces deseos
paredes pasan.»
Acercóse el caballero,
y ella, confusa y turbada,
hacer quiso celosías
de las intricadas ramas;
mas como quien tiene amor
los mares y las montañas
atraviesa fácilmente,
la dice tales palabras:
«¿Para qué te ascondes,
niña gallarda?
Que mis linces deseos
paredes pasan.»

Salen el COMENDADOR, FLORES, ORTUÑO *y* CIMBRANOS.

COM.:	Estése la boda queda,
	y no se alborote nadie.
JUAN:	No es juego aqueste, señor,
	y basta que tú lo mandes.
	¿Quieres lugar? ¿Cómo vienes
	con tu belicoso alarde?

	for both you and Frondoso.
EST.:	Rojo, I pray that heaven gives its hand
	to her and her husband
	with its plentiful blessing.
FRO.:	Both of you, bless us both.
JUAN:	Come on, play your instruments and sing,
	because they've been joined together.
MUS.:	"To the valley of Fuenteovejuna

the maiden with unbound hair descends;
she is followed by the knight
with the Cross of Calatrava.
She hides amid the shrubbery,
ashamed and dismayed;
pretending she hasn't seen him,
she screens herself with the branches.
   'Why are you hiding,
elegant girl?
For my lynx-eyed desires
can through walls.'
   The knight approached,
and she, confused and dismayed,
tried to make shutters
out of the entangled branches;
but, since a man in love
easily crosses
seas and mountains,
he spoke these words to her:
   'Why are you hiding,
elegant girl?
For my lynx-eyed desires
can see through walls.'"

Enter the COMMANDER, FLORES, ORTUÑO, *and* CIMBRANOS.

COM.:	Let the wedding party remain calm;
	nobody get upset.
JUAN:	This isn't a game, sir,
	and it's enough that you command it.
	Would you like a seat? How is it you come
	in such warlike array?

          ¿Venciste? Mas ¿qué pregunto?

FRO.:   ¡Muerto soy! ¡Cielos, libradme!

LAU.:   Huye por aquí, Frondoso.

COM.:   Eso no; prendelde, atalde.

JUAN: Date, muchacho, a prisión.

FRO.:   Pues ¿quieres tú que me maten?

JUAN: ¿Por qué?

COM.:   No soy hombre yo
       que mato sin culpa a nadie;
       que si lo fuera, le hubieran
       pasado de parte a parte
       esos soldados que traigo.
       Llevarle mando a la cárcel,
       donde la culpa que tiene
       sentencie su mismo padre.

PAS.:   Señor, mirad que se casa.

COM.:   ¿Qué me obliga a que se case?
       ¿No hay otra gente en el pueblo?

PAS.:   Si os ofendió, perdonadle,
       por ser vos quien sois.

COM.:   No es cosa,
       Pascuala, en que yo soy parte.
       Es esto contra el maestre
       Téllez Girón, que Dios guarde;
       es contra toda su orden,
       es su honor, y es importante
       para el ejemplo el castigo;
       que habrá otro día quien trate
       de alzar pendón contra él,
       pues ya sabéis que una tarde
       al comendador mayor
       (¡qué vasallos tan leales!)
       puso una ballesta al pecho.

[margin handwritten note: Honor / challenge of teragura]

EST.:   Supuesto que el disculparle
       ya puede tocar a un suegro,
       no es mucho que en causas tales
       se descomponga con vos
       un hombre, en efeto, amante;
       porque si vos pretendéis
       su propia mujer quitarle,

	Did you win the battle? But why do I even ask?
Fro.:	I'm a dead man! Heaven, save me!
Lau.:	Flee through here, Frondoso!
Com.:	No, he won't! Seize him, tie him up!
Juan:	My boy, submit to being a prisoner.
Fro.:	Why? Do you want me to be killed?
Juan:	Why do you say that?
Com.:	I'm not a man

who kills anyone that's innocent;
if I were, he would have been
run through
by these soldiers I have with me.
I order him to be taken to prison,
where his own father can sentence him
for the crime he has committed.

Pas.:	My lord, please observe that this is his wedding.
Com.:	Why should I care about his getting married?
	Aren't there other men in town?
Pas.:	If he offended you, forgive him,
	because you are such a great man.
Com.:	It's not a matter,

Pascuala, that concerns me personally.
His crime is against the Master,
Téllez Girón (whom God protect);
it's against his entire Order,
it touches on his honor, and it's important
for punishment to be meted out as an example;
or else at some later date someone will try
to rebel against him,
since you know that, one afternoon
he placed a crossbow to the breast
of his Chief Commander
(such loyal vassals!).

| Est.: | If the power of excusing him |

can fall to the lot of a father-in-law,
it's no wonder that, in such situations,
a man who is truly in love
might lose his temper with you;
because if you attempt
to take away his own wife,

¿qué mucho que la defienda?

COM.: Majadero sois, alcalde.

EST.: Por vuestra virtud, señor.

COM.: Nunca yo quise quitarle
su mujer, pues no lo era.

EST.: Sí quisistes . . . Y esto baste;
que reyes hay en Castilla
que nuevas órdenes hacen,
con que desórdenes quitan.   *Jeraquía*
Y harán mal, cuando descansen
de las guerras, en sufrir
en sus villas y lugares
a hombres tan poderosos,
por traer cruces tan grandes.
Póngasela el rey al pecho,
que para pechos reales
es esa insignia, y no más.

COM.: ¡Hola! La vara quitalde.

EST.: Tomad, señor, norabuena.

COM.: Pues con ella quiero dalle,
como a caballo brïoso.

EST.: Por señor os sufro. Dadme.

PAS.: ¡A un viejo de palos das!

LAU.: Si le das porque es mi padre,
¿qué vengas en él de mí?

COM.: Llevadla, y haced que guarden
su persona diez soldados.

Vase él, y los suyos.

EST.: ¡Justicia del cielo baje!

Vase.

W 1642

PAS.: ¡Volvióse en luto la boda!
" Mourning "
Vase.

lutar esas
personas
metaforica...
están muertos

BAR.: ¿No hay aquí un hombre que hable?

MEN.: Yo tengo ya mis azotes,

is it surprising that he should defend her?

COM.: You're speaking foolishly, Mayor.

EST.: On behalf of your virtue, my lord.

COM.: I never tried to take away
his wife, because she wasn't.

EST.: Yes, you did . . . But, enough said;
for there are monarchs in Castile
who are creating new order and Orders,
in order to eliminate disorder.
And they'll do wrong if, once their
wars are over, they permit
in their cities and towns
men who are so powerful
because they wear such a big Cross.
Let the King put it on his own breast,
because that emblem befits
a royal breast, and no other.

COM.: Soldiers! Take away his staff of office!

EST.: Take it, my lord, and welcome to it!

COM.: Because I want to beat him with it
like an unruly horse.

EST.: Since you're my lord, I allow it. Beat me!

PAS.: You're striking an old man?!

LAU.: If you're beating him because he's my father,
why are you taking revenge on him for what I did?

COM.: Seize her, and see that she's
guarded by ten soldiers!

He and his men exit.

EST.: May justice descend from heaven!

He exits.

PAS.: The wedding has turned into a funeral! *Oh no!*

She exits.

BAR.: Is there no man here who will speak up?

MEN.: I already have my whipping;

que aun se ven los cardenales
sin que un hombre vaya a Roma.
Prueben otros a enojarle.

JUAN: Hablemos todos.

MEN.:   Señores,
aquí todo el mundo calle:
¡como ruedas de salmón
me puso los atabales!

the contusions, red as cardinals' robes,[34] can still be seen
without the necessity of visiting Rome.
Let other people try to rile him up.

JUAN: Let's all speak up!

MEN.:   Gentlemen,
let everyone remain silent here:
he made my behind
look like slices of salmon!

---

34. In Spanish, the same word means "contusion" and "cardinal."

Acto tercero

Salen ESTEBAN, ALONSO *y* BARRILDO.

EST.: ¿No han venido a la junta?
BAR.:   No han venido.
EST.: Pues más apriesa nuestro daño corre.
BAR.: Ya está lo más del pueblo prevenido.
EST.: Frondoso con prisiones en la torre,
y mi hija Laurencia en tanto aprieto,
si la piedad de Dios no lo socorre . . .

Salen JUAN ROJO *y el* REGIDOR.

JUAN: ¿De qué dais voces, cuando importa tanto
a nuestro bien, Esteban, el secreto?
EST.: Que doy tan pocas es mayor espanto.

Sale MENGO.

MEN.: También vengo a hallarme en esta junta.
EST.: Un hombre cuyas canas baña el llanto,
labradores honrados, os pregunta
    qué obsequias debe hacer toda esta gente
a su patria sin honra, ya perdida.
Y si se llaman honras justamente,
    ¿cómo se harán, si no hay entre nosotros
hombre a quien este bárbaro no afrente?
Respondedme: ¿hay alguno de vosotros
    que no esté lastimado en honra y vida?
¿No os lamentáis los unos de los otros?

102

Act Three

Enter ESTEBAN, ALONSO, *and* BARRILDO.

EST.: Haven't they come to the meeting?
BAR.:   They haven't come.
EST.: Then, harm is approaching us more rapidly.
BAR.: Most of the town has already been notified.
EST.:   Frondoso in shackles in the tower,
and my daughter Laurencia in such straits—
if God's mercy doesn't help us . . .

Enter JUAN ROJO *and the* COUNCILMAN.

JUAN: Why are you crying out, Esteban, when secrecy
is so essential to our well-being?
EST.: It's a greater wonder that I cry out so little.

Enter MENGO.

MEN.: I have come, too, to take part in this meeting.
EST.: A man whose gray hairs are soaked in tears
asks you, honorable husbandmen,
   what sort of funeral service all of us should perform
for our native town which is dishonored and now ruined.
And if a funeral is rightly called "showing honor,"
   how can it be held if there is no man
among us whom this barbarian is not insulting?
Answer me: is there one of you
   who isn't injured in his honor or his person?
Aren't all of you lamenting for one another?

103

＊ 3 opciones

Pues si ya la tenéis todos perdida,
    ¿a qué aguardáis? ¿Qué desventura es esta?

JUAN: La mayor que en el mundo fue sufrida.
Mas pues ya se publica y manifiesta
    que en paz tienen los reyes a Castilla,
y su venida a Córdoba se apresta,
vayan dos regidores de la villa,
    y, echándose a sus pies, pidan remedio.

BAR.:   En tanto que Fernando, aquel que humilla
a tantos enemigos, otro medio
    será mejor, pues no podrá, ocupado,
hacernos bien, con tanta guerra en medio.

REG.:   Si mi voto de vos fuera escuchado,
    desamparar la villa doy por voto.

JUAN: ¿Cómo es posible en tiempo limitado?

MEN.:   ¡A la fe, que si entiende el alboroto,
    que ha de costar la junta alguna vida!

REG.:   Ya, todo el árbol de paciencia roto,
corre la nave de temor perdida.
    La hija quitan con tan gran fiereza
a un hombre honrado, de quien es regida
la patria en que vivís, y en la cabeza
    la vara quiebran tan injustamente.
¿Qué esclavo se trató con más bajeza?

JUAN: ¿Qué es lo que quieres tú que el pueblo intente?

REG.:   Morir, o dar la muerte a los tiranos,
    pues somos muchos, y ellos poca gente.

BAR.:   ¡Contra el señor las armas en las manos!

EST.:   El rey sólo es señor después del cielo,
y no bárbaros hombres inhumanos.
Si Dios ayuda nuestro justo celo,
    ¿qué nos ha de costar?

MEN.:   Mirad, señores,
que vais en estas cosas con recelo.
Puesto que por los simples labradores
    estoy aquí, que más injurias pasan,
más cuerdo represento sus temores.

JUAN: Si nuestras desventuras se compasan,
    para perder las vidas, ¿qué aguardamos?
Las casas y las viñas nos abrasan:
tiranos son. ¡A la venganza vamos!

	Then, if all of you have lost your honor,
	what are you waiting for? What misfortune is this?
JUAN:	The greatest ever suffered in the world.
	But, since it is already proclaimed and manifested
	that the two monarchs have pacified Castile
	and their arrival in Córdoba is imminent,
	let two town councilmen visit them
	and, throwing themselves at their feet, ask for redress.
BAR.:	Until King Fernando, who humbles
	so many enemies, can arrive, it will be better
	to seek other means, because, occupied as he is, he won't be able
	to help us, with so many wars impeding him.
COU.:	If you were to listen to my suggestion,
	I vote that we evacuate the town.
JUAN:	How is that possible in such a limited time?
MEN.:	By my faith, if he gets wind of our disturbance,
	it will surely cost the lives of some at this meeting!
COU.:	By now, the mast of our patience is entirely shattered
	and our ship is sailing frenzied with fear.
	With such great ferocity they abduct the daughter
	of a respectable man, who governs
	the town in which you live, and on his head
	they break his staff of office so unjustly!
	What slave was ever treated more basely?
JUAN:	What is it you want the people to attempt?
COU.:	To die, or put the tyrants to death,
	for we are many and they are few.
BAR.:	An armed uprising against our lord!
EST.:	The King alone is lord, after heaven,
	and not inhuman, barbarous men.
	If God aids our just enthusiasm,
	what can it cost us?
MEN.:	See to it, gentlemen,
	that you proceed cautiously in these matters.
	Because I here represent
	the lowly peasants, who are undergoing more injuries,
	I speak more wisely about their fears.
JUAN:	If our misfortunes increase at the same rate,
	what fear of losing our lives holds us back?
	They're burning our houses and vineyards:
	they're tyrants. Let's avenge ourselves!

Sale LAURENCIA, *desmelenada.*

LAU.:   Dejadme entrar, que bien puedo
en consejo de los hombres;
que bien puede una mujer,
si no a dar voto, a dar voces.
¿Conocéisme?

EST.:   ¡Santo cielo!
¿No es mi hija?

JUAN: ¿No conoces
a Laurencia?

LAU.:   Vengo tal,
que mi diferencia os pone
en contingencia quién soy.

EST.:   ¡Hija mía!

LAU.:   No me nombres
tu hija.

EST.:   ¿Por qué, mis ojos?
¿Por qué?

LAU.:   Por muchas razones,
y sean las principales,
porque dejas que me roben
tiranos sin que me vengues,
traidores sin que me cobres.
Aún no era yo de Frondoso,
para que digas que tome,
como marido, venganza,
que aquí por tu cuenta corre;
que en tanto que de las bodas
no haya llegado la noche,
del padre, y no del marido,
la obligación presupone;
que en tanto que no me entregan
una joya, aunque la compre,
no ha de correr por mi cuenta
las guardas ni los ladrones.
Llevóme de vuestros ojos
a su casa Fernán Gómez:
la oveja al lobo dejáis,
como cobardes pastores.
¡Qué dagas no vi en mi pecho!

Enter LAURENCIA, *disheveled.*

LAU.:   Let me in, for I have a right
to join a council of men;
for a woman may well attend,
if not to vote, at least to give voice to her distress.
Do you recognize me?

EST.:   Dear heaven!
Aren't you my daughter?

JUAN: You don't recognize
Laurencia?

LAU.:   I'm in such a state
that the change in me makes you
unsure who I am.

EST.:   My daughter!

LAU.:   Don't call me
your daughter.

EST.:   Why not, my precious one?
Why not?

LAU.:   For many reasons.
To name just the main ones:
because you allow me to be abducted
by tyrants without avenging me,
by traitors without reclaiming me.
I did not yet belong to Frondoso,
so you can't say that, as my husband,
he should have taken revenge;
the revenge was owed by you;
because, as long as the wedding
night hasn't arrived,
the father and not the husband
is assumed to have the obligation;
until a jewel is handed over
to me, even though I've paid for it,
I shouldn't be responsible
for the security guards or the thieves.
In front of your eyes Fernán Gómez
carried me off to his house;
you abandoned the sheep to the wolf
like cowardly shepherds.
All the daggers I saw at my breast!

¡Qué desatinos enormes,
qué palabras, qué amenazas,
y qué delitos atroces,
por rendir mi castidad
a sus apetitos torpes!
¿Mis cabellos no lo dicen?
¿No se ven aquí los golpes
de la sangre y las señales?
¿Vosotros sois hombres nobles?
¿Vosotros, padres y deudos?
¿Vosotros, que no se os rompen
las entrañas de dolor,
de verme en tantos dolores?
Ovejas sois, bien lo dice
de Fuenteovejuna el nombre.
Dadme unas armas a mí,   ——→ *Yo y las mujeres*
pues sois piedras, pues sois bronces,
pues sois jaspes, pues sois tigres . . .
Tigres no, porque feroces
siguen quien roba sus hijos,
matando los cazadores
antes que entren por el mar
y por sus ondas se arrojen.
Liebres cobardes nacisteis;
bárbaros sois, no españoles.
Gallinas, ¡vuestras mujeres
sufrís que otros hombres gocen!
¡Poneos ruecas en la cinta!
¿Para qué os ceñís estoques?
¡Vive Dios, que he de trazar
que solas mujeres cobren   *HONOR: Las mujeres*
la honra de estos tiranos,   *Sufriendo de los*
la sangre de estos traidores!   *hombres tiranos*
¡Y que os han de tirar piedras,
hilanderas, maricones,   *—Su enojo está*
amujerados, cobardes!   *Justificado*
¡Y que mañana os adornen
nuestras tocas y basquiñas,
solimanes y colores!

All the horrible absurdities,
all the speeches, all the threats,
and all the awful crimes,
so that I would yield my chastity
to his foul lusts!
Doesn't my hair tell you the story?
Can't you see here the clots
of blood and the bruises?
You call yourselves upright men?
You call yourselves fathers and kinsmen?
You, whose hearts
aren't breaking with sorrow
to see me in so many sorrows?
You're sheep, the name
of Fuenteovejuna tells it plainly.[35]
Give some weapons to me,
since you're just lumps of stone, of bronze,
of jasper, since you're as cruel as tigers . . .
No, you're not tigers, because *they* ferociously
pursue the abductor of their young,
killing the hunters
before they can put out to sea,
launching their boat on its waves.
You were born cowardly hares;
you're barbarians, not Spaniards!
Chicken-hearts, you allow
other men to enjoy your women!
Put distaffs in your belts!
Why do you gird on rapiers?
As God lives, I'll have to arrange
for only women to regain
their honor from these tyrants,
their blood from these traitors!
And at you they'll shy stones,
you spinning-girls, you unmanly,
effeminate cowards!
And tomorrow may you be adorned
with our headdresses and skirts,
our cosmetics and rouge!

35. On this incorrect folk etymology, see the Introduction.

A Frondoso quiere ya,
sin sentencia, sin pregones,
colgar el comendador
del almena de una torre:
de todos hará lo mismo;
y yo me huelgo, medio-hombres,
por que quede sin mujeres
esta villa honrada, y torne
aquel siglo de amazonas,
eterno espanto del orbe.

EST.:   Yo, hija, no soy de aquellos
que permiten que los nombres
con esos títulos viles.
Iré solo, si se pone
todo el mundo contra mí.

JUAN: Y yo, por más que me asombre
la grandeza del contrario.

REG.:   Muramos todos.

BAR.:   Descoge
un lienzo al viento en un palo,
y mueran estos inormes.

JUAN: ¿Qué orden pensáis tener?

MEN.:   Ir a matarle sin orden.
Juntad el pueblo a una voz,
que todos están conformes
en que los tiranos mueran.

EST.:   Tomad espadas, lanzones,
ballestas, chuzos y palos.

MEN.:   ¡Los reyes nuestros señores
vivan!

TODOS: ¡Vivan muchos años!

MEN.:   ¡Mueran tiranos traidores!

TODOS: ¡Traidores tiranos mueran!

Vanse todos.

LAU.:   Caminad, que el cielo os oye.
¡Ah, mujeres de la villa!
¡Acudid, por que se cobre
vuestro honor, acudid todas!

Without a formal sentence, without a public announcement,
the Commander now wishes
to hang Frondoso
from the battlements of a tower:
he'll do the same to everyone,
and I'm glad of it, you half-men;
that way, this honorable town will be left
without women like you, and the age
of Amazons will return,
an eternal wonder of the world.

EST.: Daughter, I am not one of those
who allow themselves to be called
such despicable names.
I'll go alone, even if
the whole world opposes me.

JUAN: So will I, no matter how much
the greatness of my opponent awes me.

COU.: Let's all die!

BAR.:   Unfurl
a banner to the wind on a pole,
and let these monsters die!

JUAN: What order do you think should be observed?

MEN.: We should go and kill him without being orderly.
Assemble the people with one proclamation,
because they all agree
that the tyrants should die!

EST.: Take swords, short spears,
crossbows, pikes, and cudgels!

MEN.: Long live the two monarchs,
our lords!

ALL: May they live many years!

MEN.: Death to tyrants and traitors!

ALL: To traitors and tyrants, death!

They all exit [except LAURENCIA].

LAU.: Go your way, because heaven hears you!
Oh, women of the town,
come here to me, in order to regain
your honor, come one and all!

Salen PASCUALA, JACINTA *y otras mujeres.*

PAS.:   ¿Qué es esto? ¿De qué das voces?

LAU.:   ¿No veis cómo todos van
          a matar a Fernán Gómez,
          y hombres, mozos y muchachos,
          furiosos, al hecho corren?
          ¿Será bien que solos ellos
          de esta hazaña el honor gocen,
          pues no son de las mujeres
          sus agravios los menores?

JAC.:   Di, pues, ¿qué es lo que pretendes?

LAU.:   Que puestas todas en orden,
          acometamos un hecho
          que dé espanto a todo el orbe.
          Jacinta, tu grande agravio
          que sea cabo; responde
          de una escuadra de mujeres.

JAC.:   No son los tuyos menores.

LAU.:   Pascuala, alférez serás.

PAS.:   Pues déjame que enarbole
          en un asta la bandera:
          verás si merezco el nombre.

LAU.:   No hay espacio para eso,
          pues la dicha nos socorre:
          bien nos basta que llevemos
          nuestras tocas por pendones.

PAS.:   Nombremos un capitán.

LAU.:   Eso no.

PAS.:   ¿Por qué?

LAU.:   Que adonde
          asiste mi gran valor,
          no hay Cides ni Rodamontes.

                    Vanse.

Enter PASCUALA, JACINTA, *and other women.*

PAS.:   What's going on? What are you shouting about?

LAU.:   Don't you see that they're all going
to kill Fernán Gómez,
and that men, lads, and boys
are running furiously to do the deed?
Is it right for them alone
to enjoy the honor of this exploit,
seeing that the injuries done to us women
are not the least of all?

JAC.:   Then, speak up, what are you suggesting?

LAU.:   That we all form ranks
and undertake a deed
that will fill the whole world with awe.
Jacinta, let the great injury done to you
take the lead; be in charge
of a squad of women!

JAC.:   Those done to you aren't slighter.

LAU.:   Pascuala, you'll be our standard-bearer.

PAS.:   Then, let me hoist
our banner on a spear:
you'll see whether I deserve the title.

LAU.:   There's no time for that,
since good luck is coming to our aid;
it's enough if we carry
our headdresses as pennants.

PAS.:   Let's appoint a captain!

LAU.:   No.

PAS.:   Why not?

LAU.:   Because where
my great valor is present,
there's no need for a Cid or a Rodomonte.[36]

All exit.

---

36. The Cid is Spain's national military hero; Rodomonte is the brave king of Algiers
in Ariosto's *Orlando furioso* whose boastfulness gave the English language the word
"rodomontade."

Sale FRONDOSO, *atadas las manos;* FLORES, ORTUÑO,
y CIMBRANOS *y el* COMENDADOR.

COM.:   De ese cordel que de las manos sobra
          quiero que le colguéis, por mayor pena.
FRO.:   ¿Qué nombre, gran señor, tu sangre cobra?

COM.:   Colgalde luego en la primera almena.
FRO.:   Nunca fue mi intención poner por obra
          tu muerte entonces.
FLO.:   Grande ruido suena.

Ruido suene.

COM.:   ¿Ruido?
FLO.:   Y de manera que interrompen
          tu justicia, señor.
ORT.:   Las puertas rompen.

Ruido.

COM.:   ¡La puerta de mi casa, y siendo casa
          de la encomienda!
FLO.:   El pueblo junto viene.

Dentro.

JUAN: ¡Rompe, derriba, hunde, quema, abrasa!
ORT.:   Un popular motín mal se detiene.
COM.:   ¿El pueblo contra mí?
FLO.:   La furia pasa
          tan adelante, que las puertas tiene
          echadas por la tierra.
COM.:   Desatalde.
          Templa, Frondoso, ese villano alcalde.
FRO.:   Yo voy, señor, que amor les ha movido.

Vase.
Dentro.

MEN.:   ¡Vivan Fernando y Isabel, y mueran
          los traidores!

Enter FRONDOSO, *with his hands tied,* FLORES, ORTUÑO,
CIMBRANOS, *and the* COMMANDER.

COM.:   With the rope left over from tying his hands
          I want him hanged, as a more severe punishment.
FRO.:   Great lord, what kind of reputation are you leaving for your
                descendants?
COM.:   Hang him at once from the nearest merlon.
FRO.:   It was never my intention actually to kill you
          on that occasion.
FLO.:   I hear a lot of noise.

Noise is heard.

COM.:   Noise?
FLO.:   And of a kind that means they are interrupting
          your justice, my lord.
ORT.:   They're breaking down the doors.

Noise.

COM.:   The door to my house, which is the seat
          of the commandery!
FLO.:   The townspeople are coming all together.

Voices are heard within.

JUAN: Smash, demolish, destroy, burn, set ablaze!
ORT.:   An uprising of the people is hard to restrain.
COM.:   The people against me?
FLO.:   Their fury is going
          so far that they've thrown
          the doors to the ground.
COM.:   Untie him!
          Frondoso, placate this peasant of a mayor! *Scared!*
FRO.:   I'll go, my lord, because their love for me has incited them.

Exit.
Voices within.

MEN.:   Long live Fernando and Isabel, and death
          to the traitors!

FLO.:   Señor, por Dios te pido
que no te hallen aquí.
COM.:   Si perseveran,
este aposento es fuerte y defendido.
Ellos se volverán.
FLO.:   Cuando se alteran
los pueblos agraviados, y resuelven,
nunca sin sangre o sin venganza vuelven.
COM.:   En esta puerta así como rastrillo,
su furor con las armas defendamos.

Dentro.

FRO.:   ¡Viva Fuenteovejuna!
COM.:   ¡Qué caudillo!
Estoy por que a su furia acometamos.
FLO.:   De la tuya, señor, me maravillo.
EST.:   Ya el tirano y los cómplices miramos.
¡Fuenteovejuna, y los tiranos mueran!

Salen todos.

COM.:   ¡Pueblo, esperad!
TODOS: ¡Agravios nunca esperan!
COM.:   Decídmelos a mí, que iré pagando
a fe de caballero esos errores.
TODOS: ¡Fuenteovejuna! ¡Viva el rey Fernando!
¡Mueran malos cristianos y traidores!
COM.:   ¿No me queréis oír? Yo estoy hablando,
yo soy vuestro señor.
TODOS: ¡Nuestros señores
son los Reyes Católicos!
COM.:   Espera.
TODOS: ¡Fuenteovejuna, y Fernán Gómez muera!

Vanse, y salen las mujeres armadas.

LAU.:   Parad en este puesto de esperanzas,
soldados atrevidos, no mujeres.
PAS.:   ¡Lo que mujeres son en las venganzas!
En él beban su sangre es bien que esperes.

FLO.:   My lord, for God's sake I beg you,
don't let them find you here!
COM.:   If they persist,
this room is strong and fortified.
They'll turn back.
FLO.:   When insulted people
lose their temper and become determined,
they never turn back without blood and vengeance.
COM.:   At this doorway, as if it were a portcullis,
let us ward off their furor with our weapons!

Voices within.

FRO.:   Long live Fuenteovejuna!
COM.:   Some captain!
My vote is for us to attack their fury.
FLO.:   My lord, I'm amazed at *yours*!
EST.:   We can now see the tyrant and his accomplices.
"Fuenteovejuna!" and let the tyrants die!

They all enter.

COM.:   Townspeople, wait!
ALL: Insults never wait!
COM.:   Tell me about them, and, on my honor as a knight,
I'll make up these mistakes to you.
ALL: Fuenteovejuna! Long live King Fernando!
Death to bad Christians and traitors!
COM.:   Won't you hear me out? I'm talking to you,
I, your lord.
ALL: Our lords
are the Catholic Monarchs!
COM.:   Wait!
ALL: Fuenteovejuna, and death to Fernán Gómez!

All exit. Enter the women, with weapons.

LAU.:   Halt in this waiting-place,
my daring soldiers, and not women!
PAS.:   What women are like when taking revenge!
In this place, you can expect them to drink his blood!

JAC.:   Su cuerpo recojamos en las lanzas.
PAS.:   Todas son de esos mismos pareceres.

Dentro.

EST.:   ¡Muere, traidor comendador!
COM.:   Ya muero.
          ¡Piedad, Señor, que en tu clemencia espero!

Dentro.

BAR.:   Aquí está Flores.
MEN.:   Dale a ese bellaco,
          que ese fue el que me dio dos mil azotes.

Dentro.

FRO.:   No me vengo, si el alma no le saco.
LAU.:   No excusamos entrar.
PAS.:   No te alborotes.
          Bien es guardar la puerta.

Dentro.

BAR.:   No me aplaco.
          ¡Con lágrimas agora, marquesotes!
LAU.:   Pascuala, yo entro dentro, que la espada
          no ha de estar tan sujeta ni envainada.

Vase.

BAR.:   Aquí está Ortuño.
FRO.:   Córtale la cara.

Sale FLORES, *huyendo, y* MENGO, *tras él.*

FLO.:   ¡Mengo, piedad, que no soy yo el culpado!
MEN.:   Cuando ser alcahuete no bastara,
          bastaba haberme el pícaro azotado.
PAS.:   Dánoslo a las mujeres, Mengo. ¡Para,
          acaba por tu vida!

JAC.:   Let's receive his body on our lances!

PAS.:   They're all of the same opinion.

Voices within.

EST.:   Die, traitorous Commander!

COM.:   I'm dying!

Mercy, O Lord, for I trust in Your clemency!

Voices within.

BAR.:   Here is Flores.

MEN.:   Give it to that rogue,

for it was he who gave me two thousand lashes.

Voices within.

FRO.:   I won't be avenged if I don't take the soul out of him.

LAU.:   Let's not hesitate to go in!

PAS.:   Don't get upset!

It's a good idea to guard this door.

Voices within.

BAR.:   I won't be placated!

Your turn to weep, lordlings!

LAU.:   Pascuala, I'm going in, because my sword

mustn't be so submissive and kept in its sheath.

Exit.

BAR.:   Here is Ortuño.

FRO.:   Cut up his face!

Enter FLORES, *fleeing, with* MENGO *behind him.*

FLO.:   Mengo, mercy! I'm not to blame!

MEN.:   Even if being a pimp weren't enough,

it would be enough for that scoundrel to have whipped me!

PAS.:   Hand him over to us women, Mengo! Halt,

stop, by your life!

MEN.:   Ya está dado;
que no le quiero yo mayor castigo.
PAS.:   Vengaré tus azotes.
MEN.:   Eso digo.
JAC.:   ¡Ea, muera el traidor!
FLO.:   ¡Entre mujeres!
JAC.:   ¿No le viene muy ancho?
PAS.:   ¿Aqueso lloras?
JAC.:   Muere, concertador de sus placeres.
PAS.:   ¡Ea, muera el traidor!
FLO.:   ¡Piedad, señoras!

Sale ORTUÑO, *huyendo de* LAURENCIA.

ORT.:   Mira que no soy yo . . .
LAU.:   ¡Ya sé quién eres!
Entrad, teñid las armas vencedoras
en estos viles.
PAS.:   Moriré matando.
TODAS: ¡Fuenteovejuna, y viva el rey Fernando!

Vanse, y salen el REY FERNANDO *y la* REINA ISABEL
y DON MANRIQUE, MAESTRE.

MAN.:   De modo la prevención
fue, que el efeto esperado
llegamos a ver logrado
con poca contradición.
        Hubo poca resistencia;
y supuesto que la hubiera,
sin duda ninguna fuera
de poca o ninguna esencia.
        Queda el de Cabra ocupado
en conservación del puesto,
por si volviere dispuesto
a él el contrario osado.
REY: Discreto el acuerdo fue,
y que asista es conveniente,
y reformando la gente,
el paso tomado esté;
        que con eso se asegura

MEN.:   He's now handed over,
            because I wish no greater punishment on him.
PAS.:   I'll avenge your whipping.
MEN.:   That's what I want.
JAC.:   Come on, let the traitor die!
FLO.:   At the hands of women?!
JAC.:   Isn't that too great an honor for him?
PAS.:   You're complaining of that?
JAC.:   Die, you pander to his pleasures!
PAS.:   Come on, let the traitor die!
FLO.:   Mercy, ladies!

            Enter ORTUÑO, *fleeing from* LAURENCIA.

ORT.:   Look, it wasn't me . . .
LAU.:   I know who you are!
            Go in, and stain your victorious weapons
            with their base blood!
PAS.:   I'll die killing.
ALL: Fuenteovejuna! And long live King Fernando!   Yee-haw!

            Exit. Enter KING FERNANDO, QUEEN ISABEL,
            and DON MANRIQUE, *the Master of Santiago.*

MAN.:   Our preparations were
            such that we have seen
            the desired effect achieved
            with little resistance.
                There was not much opposition;
            and even if there had been any,
            without a doubt it would have been
            of little or no consequence.
                The Count of Cabra is busy
            holding the fortress,
            in case our bold opponent
            should return, attempting to retake it.
KING: The plan was a wise one,
            and it's expedient for him to remain there,
            regaining the people's allegiance
            and controlling the passage between realms;
                because, that way, we can be sure

no podernos hacer mal
Alfonso, que en Portugal
tomar la fuerza procura.
   Y el de Cabra es bien que esté
en ese sitio asistente,
y como tan diligente,
muestras de su valor dé;
   porque con esto asegura
el daño que nos recela,
y como fiel centinela,
el bien del reino procura.

Sale FLORES, *herido.*

FLO.:   Católico rey Fernando,
a quien el cielo concede
la corona de Castilla,
como a varón excelente:
oye la mayor crueldad
que se ha visto entre las gentes,
desde donde nace el sol
hasta donde se escurece.
REY: Repórtate.
FLO.:   Rey supremo,
mis heridas no consienten
dilatar el triste caso,
por ser mi vida tan breve.
De Fuenteovejuna vengo,
donde, con pecho inclemente,
los vecinos de la villa
a su señor dieron muerte.
Muerto Fernán Gómez queda
por sus súbditos aleves;
que vasallos indignados
con leve causa se atreven.
Con título de tirano
que le acumula la plebe,
a la fuerza de esta voz
el hecho fiero acometen;

that we'll receive no harm
from Alfonso, who, back in Portugal,
is planning to regain power.[37]
    And it's good for Cabra to remain
operative in that place,
and, with his usual diligence,
    to display his merit;
because he will thereby avoid
the harm that we fear,
and, as a loyal sentinel,
will procure the good of the kingdom.

Enter FLORES, *wounded.*   *They let him get away?!*

FLO.:   Catholic King Fernando,
to whom heaven grants
the crown of Castile
thanks to your manly excellence:
hear the greatest cruelty
ever seen among nations,
from the place where the sun rises
to the place where it grows dark!

KING: Calm yourself.

FLO.:   Supreme King,
my wounds do not permit me
to tell the sad event at length,
because my life is nearing its end.
I have come from Fuenteovejuna,
where, with merciless hearts,
the inhabitants of the town
have put their lord to death.
Fernán Gómez has been killed
by his treacherous subjects;
because indignant vassals
become bold with a slight reason.
He was labeled a tyrant
by the common people,
and, on the strength of that appellation,
they committed the fierce deed;

---

37. Or: "retake the fortress" (Ciudad Real).

y quebrantando su casa,
no atendiendo a que se ofrece
por la fe de caballero
a que pagará a quien debe,
no sólo no le escucharon,
pero con furia impaciente
rompen el cruzado pecho
con mil heridas crüeles,
y por las altas ventanas
le hacen que al suelo vuele,
adonde en picas y espadas
le recogen las mujeres.
Llévanle a una casa muerto,
y, a porfía, quien más puede
mesa su barba y cabello
y apriesa su rostro hieren.
En efeto, fue la furia
tan grande que en ellos crece,
que las mayores tajadas
las orejas a ser vienen.
Sus armas borran con picas,
y a voces dicen que quieren
tus reales armas fijar,
porque aquellas les ofenden.
Saqueáronle la casa,
cual si de enemigos fuese,
y gozosos, entre todos
han repartido sus bienes.
Lo dicho he visto escondido,
porque mi infelice suerte
en tal trance no permite
que mi vida se perdiese;
y así estuve todo el día
hasta que la noche viene,
y salir pude escondido
para que cuenta te diese.
Haz, señor, pues eres justo,
que la justa pena lleven
de tan riguroso caso
los bárbaros delincuentes:
mira que su sangre a voces

breaking into his house,
and not heeding his offers,
made on the honor of a knight,
to make good all his debts to them,
not only did they refuse to listen to him,
but with impatient fury
they pierced his Cross-bearing breast
with a thousand cruel wounds,
and from the high windows
they made him fly to the ground,
where the women received him
on their pikes and swords.
They carried his body to a house,
where, in competition, with all their might
they plucked his beard and hair
and quickly slashed his face.
In fact, the fury
that increased within them was so great
that the largest pieces left of him
were his ears.
They obliterated his coat-of-arms with pikes,
and shouted that they wished
to display your royal arms,
because the former ones were an insult to them.
They plundered his house,
as if it belonged to an enemy,
and merrily distributed
his possessions among themselves.
I saw all that I have reported from a hiding place,
because my unhappy fate
didn't allow me to lose
my life in such a dire emergency;
and so, I remained where I was all day
until night fell
and I was able to steal away in secret
in order to give you an account of all this.
Sire, since you are just, see to it
that the barbarous criminals
receive their just punishment
for such a cruel event:
see, his blood is calling

	pide que tu rigor prueben.
REY:	Estar puedes confiado
	que sin castigo no queden.
	El triste suceso ha sido
	tal, que admirado me tiene,
	y que vaya luego un juez
	que lo averigüe conviene,
	y castigue los culpados
	para ejemplo de las gentes.
	Vaya un capitán con él,
	por que seguridad lleve;
	que tan grande atrevimiento
	castigo ejemplar requiere;
	y curad a ese soldado
	de las heridas que tiene.

Vanse, y salen los labradores y labradoras,
con la cabeza de Fernán Gómez en una lanza.

MÚS.:	*¡Muchos años vivan*
	Isabel y Fernando,
	y mueran los tiranos!
BAR.:	Diga su copla Frondoso.
FRO.:	Ya va mi copla a la fe;
	si le faltare algún pie,
	enmiéndelo el más curioso.
	«¡Vivan la bella Isabel,
	y Fernando de Aragón,
	pues que para en uno son,
	él con ella, ella con él!
	A los cielos san Miguel
	lleve a los dos de las manos.
	¡Vivan muchos años,
	y mueran los tiranos!»
LAU.:	Diga Barrildo.
BAR.:	Ya va,
	que a fe que la he pensado.
PAS.:	Si la dices con cuidado,
	buena y rebuena será.
BAR.:	*«¡Vivan los reyes famosos*
	muchos años, pues que tienen

out loud for them to feel your severe wrath.

KING: You can be assured
that they won't remain unpunished.
This sad occurrence is
such that I am lost in amazement.
A judge shall leave immediately
with the duty of confirming your report
and punishing the guilty parties
as an example to the people.
A captain shall go with him
for his safety;
for such great boldness
calls for an exemplary punishment;
cure this soldier
of the wounds he has sustained!

*Exit. Enter male and female peasants
with Fernán Gómez's head on a lance.*

MUS.:   "Long live
Isabel and Fernando,
and death to tyrants!"

BAR.:   Let Frondoso recite his refrain.

FRO.:   Here comes my refrain, by my faith;
if it's missing a syllable,
let a more careful man correct it!
"Long live beautiful Isabel
and Fernando of Aragon,
since they are a couple,
he with her she with him!
May Saint Michael lead them both
to heaven by the hand!
May they live many years,
and death to tyrants!"

LAU.:   Let Barrildo recite his.

BAR.:   Here goes,
and this time I've really put some thought into it.

PAS.:   If you recite it carefully,
it will be good, and better than good.

BAR.:   "May the famous monarchs live
many years, since they've gained

la vitoria, y a ser vienen
nuestros dueños venturosos!
¡Salgan siempre vitoriosos
de gigantes y de enanos,
y mueran los tiranos!»

MÚS.:   *¡Muchos años vivan!,* etc.

LAU.:   Diga Mengo.

FRO.:   Mengo diga.

MEN.:   Yo soy poeta donado.

PAS.:   Mejor dirás: lastimado
el envés de la barriga.

MEN.:   *«Una mañana en domingo*
me mandó azotar aquel,
de manera que el rabel
daba espantoso respingo;
pero agora que los pringo,
¡vivan los Reyes Cristiánigos,
y mueran los tiránigos!»

MÚS.:   *¡Vivan muchos años!*

EST.:   Quita la cabeza allá.

MEN.:   Cara tiene de ahorcado.

Saca un escudo JUAN ROJO *con las armas.*

REG.:   ¿Ya las armas han llegado?

EST.:   Mostrá las armas acá.

JUAN: ¿Adónde se han de poner?

REG.:   Aquí, en el ayuntamiento.

EST.:   ¡Bravo escudo!

BAR.:   ¡Qué contento!

FRO.:   Ya comienza a amanecer,
con este sol, nuestro día.

EST.:   ¡Vivan Castilla y León,
y las barras de Aragón,
y muera la tiranía!
    Advertid, Fuenteovejuna,
a las palabras de un viejo;
que el admitir su consejo
no ha dañado vez ninguna.
    Los reyes han de querer
averiguar este caso,

	the victory, and are about to become
	our luck-bringing masters!
	May they always emerge victorious
	from battles with giants and dwarves,
	and death to tyrants!"
MUS.:	"May they live many years!" [etc.]
LAU.:	Let Mengo say his.
FRO.:	Let Mengo speak.
MEN.:	As a poet, I'm only a layman.
PAS.:	You ought to say: someone
	on whose butt men lay lashes.
MEN.:	"One Sunday morning
	that man had me whipped
	so hard that my behind
	gave fearful twitches;
	but now that *I'm* beating *them,*
	long live the Christian Monarchs, oh!
	and death to tyrants, oh!"
MUS.:	"May they live many years!"
EST.:	Take the head over yonder.
MEN.:	His face is like a hanged man's.

JUAN ROJO *brings out an escutcheon with the royal arms.*

COU.:	The arms have already come?
EST.:	Show us the arms.
JUAN:	Where should they be placed?
COU.:	Here, in the town hall.
EST.:	A fine escutcheon!
BAR ·	What happinooo!
FRO.:	With this sun, our day
	is now starting to dawn.
EST.:	Long live Castile and León,
	and the bars of Aragon,
	and death to tyranny!
	Fuenteovejuna, give heed
	to an old man's words;
	because accepting his advice
	has never done any harm.
	The monarchs will surely want
	to investigate this case,

       y más tan cerca del paso
       y jornada que han de hacer.
          Concertaos todos a una
       en lo que habéis de decir.
FRO.:   ¿Qué es tu consejo?
EST.:   Morir
       diciendo «¡Fuenteovejuna!»
          Y a nadie saquen de aquí.
FRO.:   Es el camino derecho:
       Fuenteovejuna lo ha hecho.
EST.:   ¿Queréis responder así?
TODOS: Sí.
EST.:   ⚡   Ahora pues; yo quiero ser
       agora el pesquisidor,
       para ensayarnos mejor
       en lo que habemos de hacer.
          Sea Mengo el que esté puesto
       en el tormento.
MEN.:   ¿No hallaste
       otro más flaco?
EST.:   ¿Pensaste
       que era de veras?
MEN.:   Di, presto.
EST.:   ¿Quién mató al comendador?
MEN.:   ¡Fuenteovejuna lo hizo!
EST.:   Perro, ¿si te martirizo?
MEN.:   Aunque me matéis, señor.
EST.:   Confiesa, ladrón.
MEN.:   Confieso.
EST.:   Pues ¿quién fue?
MEN.:   ¡Fuenteovejuna!
EST.:   Dalde otra vuelta.
MEN.:   Es ninguna.
EST.:   Cagajón para el proceso.

                    Sale el REGIDOR.

REG.:   ¿Qué hacéis de esta suerte aquí?

and especially when they're so close to the passage between the realms
and the expedition they have to make.
   All of you, get together and agree on
what you're going to say.
FRO.:   What's your advice?
EST.:   To die
saying: "Fuenteovejuna!"
   And let everyone stick to this.
FRO.:   That is the straight path:
it *was* Fuenteovejuna that did it.
EST.:   Are you willing to give that reply?
ALL: Yes.
EST.:   Well, then, I am going to enact
the investigator's role now,
so we can better rehearse
what we have to do.
   Let Mengo be the one placed
on the rack.
MEN.:   Couldn't you find
someone more weak-willed?[38]
EST.:   Did you think
this was for real?
MEN.:   Then speak right away.
EST.:   Who killed the Commander?
MEN.:   Fuenteovejuna did it!
EST.:   Dog! What if I torture you?
MEN.:   Even if you kill me, sir.
EST.:   Confess, thief!
MEN.:   I confess.
EST.:   Well, who did it?
MEN.:   Fuenteovejuna!
EST.:   Turn the screws again!
MEN.:   It makes no difference.
EST.:   We shit on their trial!

Enter the COUNCILMAN.

COU.:   What are you doing here like this?

_____

38. The Spanish *flaco* basically means "thin." This is a joke, because, as later dialogue points out, Mengo is fat.

FRO.:	¿Qué ha sucedido, Cuadrado?
REG.:	Pesquisidor ha llegado.
EST.:	Echá todos por ahí.
REG.:	Con él viene un capitán.
EST.:	Venga el diablo: ya sabéis
	lo que responder tenéis.
REG.:	El pueblo prendiendo van,
	sin dejar alma ninguna.
EST.:	Que no hay que tener temor.
	¿Quién mató al comendador,
	Mengo?
MEN.:	¿Quién? ¡Fuenteovejuna!

Vanse, y salen el MAESTRE *y un* SOLDADO.

MAE.:	¡Que tal caso ha sucedido!
	Infelice fue su suerte.
	Estoy por darte la muerte
	por la nueva que has traído.
SOL.:	Yo, señor, soy mensajero,
	y enojarte no es mi intento.
MAE.:	¡Que a tal tuvo atrevimiento
	un pueblo enojado y fiero!
	Iré con quinientos hombres,
	y la villa he de asolar;
	en ella no ha de quedar
	ni aun memoria de los nombres.
SOL.:	Señor, tu enojo reporta;
	porque ellos al rey se han dado,
	y no tener enojado
	al rey es lo que te importa.
MAE.:	¿Cómo al rey se pueden dar,
	si de la encomienda son?
SOL.:	Con él sobre esa razón
	podrás luego pleitear.
MAE.:	¿Por pleito, cuándo salió
	lo que él le entregó en sus manos?

FRO.:   What has happened, Cuadrado?
COU.:   The investigator has arrived.
EST.:   Everyone gather over here!
COU.:   He has a captain with him.
EST.:   Let the devil come! By now you all know
        what reply you must give.
COU.:   They're arresting the townspeople,
            without omitting a soul.
EST.:   There's no need to be afraid.
        Who killed the Commander,
        Mengo?
MEN.:   Who? Fuenteovejuna!

They exit. Enter the MASTER *of Calatrava and a* SOLDIER.

MAS.:   To think that such a thing happened!
        His fate was unhappy.
        I feel like putting you to death
        for the news you have brought.
SOL.:   My lord, I'm only a messenger,
        and it wasn't my intention to vex you.
MAS.:   To think that an irritated, unruly town
        was bold enough to do that!
            I shall go there with five hundred men
        and level the town with the ground;
        there shall not remain in it
        even the memory of their names.
SOL.:   My lord, calm your anger;
        because they have turned themselves over to the King,
        and the important thing for you now
        is to avoid irritating the King.
MAS.:   How can they turn themselves over to the King
        if they belong to the commandery?
SOL.:   You can litigate with him
        later over that matter.
MAS.:   When has litigation ever released
        anything that the people placed in his hands?[39]

---

39. The ambiguity of these Spanish lines has led to a number of interpretations. Besides the one in our English text, there are: "When has litigation ever released anything that the King placed in the Commander's hands?" and "When has litigation ever released anything that the King has placed in the hands of justice?"

Son señores soberanos,
y tal reconozco yo.
     Por saber que al rey se han dado
se reportará mi enojo,
y ver su presencia escojo
por lo más bien acertado;
     que puesto que tenga culpa
en casos de gravedad,
en todo mi poca edad
viene a ser quien me disculpa.
     Con vergüenza voy; mas es
honor quien puede obligarme,
y importa no descuidarme
en tan honrado interés.

Vanse.
Sale LAURENCIA, *sola.*

LAU.:   Amando, recelar daño en lo amado,
nueva pena de amor se considera,
que quien en lo que ama daño espera
aumenta en el temor nuevo cuidado.
     El firme pensamiento desvelado,
si le aflige el temor, fácil se altera;
que no es a firme fe pena ligera
ver llevar el temor el bien robado.
     Mi esposo adoro; la ocasión que veo
al temor de su daño me condena,
si no le ayuda la felice suerte.
     Al bien suyo se inclina mi deseo:
si está presente, está cierta mi pena;
si está en ausencia, está cierta mi muerte.

Sale FRONDOSO.

FRO.:   ¡Mi Laurencia!
LAU.:   Esposo amado,
     ¿cómo a estar aquí te atreves?
FRO.:   ¿Esas resistencias debes
     a mi amoroso cuidado?
LAU.:   Mi bien, procura guardarte,

They are my sovereign lords,
and I acknowledge it.
    Knowing that they have turned themselves over to the King,
I shall calm my anger,
and I choose to see him in person
as the best thing I can do;
    because, even if I am to blame
for serious offenses,
in the whole affair my youth
will serve as my excuse.
    I go there shamefacedly; but it is
honor that obliges me to,
and it is essential not to be unwary
when my interests are so honorable.

They exit.
Enter LAURENCIA, *alone.*

LAU.:   Being in love, and fearing lest harm come to the beloved,
is to be considered a new sorrow of love,
because whoever expects that harm will come to the one he loves
gains additional worries because of his fear.
    If one's constant, vigilant concerns
are afflicted by fear, they are easily dismayed,
because it is no small sorrow to one of constant faith
to see fear make away with his happiness.
    I adore my husband; the occasion I see before me
condemns me to fear that he will be harmed,
unless a happy fate assists him.
    My desires incline toward his well-being.
if he is present, my sorrow is assured;
if he is absent, my death is assured.

Enter FRONDOSO.

FRO.:   My Laurencia!

LAU.:   Beloved husband,
how can you be so rash as to come here?

FRO.:   Does my loving concern
deserve such resistance on your part?

LAU.:   Darling, try to protect yourself,

porque tu daño recelo.

FRO.:   No quiera, Laurencia, el cielo
que tal llegue a disgustarte.

LAU.:   ¿No temes ver el rigor
que por los demás sucede,
y el furor con que procede
aqueste pesquisidor?
   Procura guardar la vida.
Huye, tu daño no esperes.

FRO.:   ¿Cómo que procure quieres
cosa tan mal recebida?
   ¿Es bien que los demás deje
en el peligro presente,
y de tu vista me ausente?
No me mandes que me aleje,
   porque no es puesto en razón
que, por evitar mi daño,
sea con mi sangre extraño
en tan terrible ocasión.

Voces dentro.

   Voces parece que he oído,
y son, si yo mal no siento,
de alguno que dan tormento.
Oye con atento oído.

Dice dentro el JUEZ, *y responden.*

JUEZ: Decid la verdad, buen viejo.
FRO.:   Un viejo, Laurencia mía,
atormentan.
LAU.:   ¡Qué porfía!
EST.:   Déjenme un poco.
JUEZ: Ya os dejo.
   Decid, ¿quién mató a Fernando?
EST.:   Fuenteovejuna lo hizo.
LAU.:   Tu nombre, padre, eternizo.
FRO.:   ¡Bravo caso!
JUEZ: Ese muchacho
aprieta. Perro, yo sé

because I fear that harm will come to you.

FRO.:   Laurencia, may it not be heaven's will
that such an occurrence gives you grief!

LAU.:   Don't you fear to witness the severity
with which the others are being treated,
and the furor with which
this investigator is proceeding?
Try to save your life.
Flee, don't wait around to be hurt.

FRO.:   How can you want me to attempt
something so unacceptable?
Is it right for me to abandon the others
in their present danger,
and to absent myself from your sight?
Don't order me to go away,
because it's unreasonable
for me, in order to avoid harm to myself,
to be a stranger to my own flesh and blood
on such a terrible occasion.

A cry within.

I thought I heard a cry,
and, if I heard correctly, it was
that of someone being tortured.
Listen with an attentive ear!

The JUDGE *speaks within, and various characters reply.*

JUD.:   Tell the truth, my good old man.

FRO.:   My Laurencia, they're torturing
an old man.

LAU.:   What persistency!

EST.:   Release me for a while.

JUD.:   I now release you.
Tell me, who killed Fernando?

EST.:   Fuenteovejuna did it.

LAU.:   Father, I immortalize your name.

FRO.:   A brave action!

JUD.:   Tighten the ropes
on that boy. Dog, I know

que lo sabes. Di quién fue.
¿Callas? Aprieta, borracho.

NIÑO: Fuenteovejuna, señor.

JUEZ: ¡Por vida del rey, villanos,
que os ahorque con mis manos!
¿Quién mató al comendador?

FRO.:   ¡Que a un niño le den tormento
y niegue de aquesta suerte!

LAU.:   ¡Bravo pueblo!

FRO.:   Bravo y fuerte.

JUEZ: Esa mujer al momento
En ese potro tened.
Dale esa mancuerda luego.

LAU.:   Ya está de cólera ciego.

JUEZ: Que os he de matar, creed,
en este potro, villanos.
¿Quién mató al comendador?

PAS.:   Fuenteovejuna, señor.

JUEZ: ¡Dale!

FRO.:   Pensamientos vanos.

LAU.:   Pascuala niega, Frondoso.

FRO.:   Niegan niños: ¿qué te espantas?

JUEZ: Parece que los encantas.
¡Aprieta!

PAS.:   ¡Ay, cielo piadoso!

JUEZ: ¡Aprieta, infame! ¿Estás sordo?

PAS.:   Fuenteovejuna lo hizo.

JUEZ: Traedme aquel más rollizo;
¡ese desnudo, ese gordo!

LAU.:   ¡Pobre Mengo! Él es sin duda.

FRO.:   Temo que ha de confesar.

MEN.:   ¡Ay, ay!

JUEZ: Comienza a apretar.

MEN.:   ¡Ay!

JUEZ: ¿Es menester ayuda?

MEN.:   ¡Ay, ay!

JUEZ: ¿Quién mató, villano,
al señor comendador?

MEN.:   ¡Ay, yo lo diré, señor!

JUEZ: Afloja un poco la mano.

FRO.:   Él confiesa.

"Fuenteovejuna lo hizo"

	that you know. Tell who it was!
	Silent? Tighten, you drunk!
BOY:	Fuenteovejuna, sir.
JUD.:	By the King's life, peasants,
	I'll hang you with my own hands!
	Who killed the Commander?
FRO.:	To think that, under torture, a mere boy
	refuses to reply this way!
LAU.:	Brave people!
FRO.:	Brave and strong.
JUD.:	Now place that woman
	on that rack!
	Give her a tug of the ropes at once!
LAU.:	By now he's blind with anger.
JUD.:	Believe me, I'm going to kill you
	on this rack, peasants.
	Who killed the Commander?
PAS.:	Fuenteovejuna, sir.
JUD.:	Tighten!
FRO.:	His words are in vain.
LAU.:	Pascuala refuses to talk, Frondoso.
FRO.:	Even children refuse. Why are you amazed?
JUD.:	You seem to be bewitching them, executioner!
	Tighter!
PAS.:	Oh, merciful heaven!
JUD.:	Tighter, you villain! Are you deaf?
PAS.:	Fuenteovejuna did it.
JUD.:	Bring me that chubbier fellow,
	that stripped one, that fat one!
LAU.:	Poor Mengo! It's surely him
FRO.:	I'm afraid he'll confess.
MEN.:	Oh! Oh!
JUD.:	Start tightening!
MEN.:	Oh!
JUD.:	You need help?
MEN.:	Oh! Oh!
JUD.:	Peasant, who killed
	the lord Commander?
MEN.:	Oh! I'll tell you, sir!
JUD.:	Loosen the ropes a little.
FRO.:	He's confessing.

JUEZ: Al palo aplica
          la espalda.
MEN.:   Quedo, que yo
          lo diré.
JUEZ: ¿Quién lo mató?
MEN.:   Señor, Fuenteovejunica.
JUEZ: ¿Hay tan gran bellaquería?
          Del dolor se están burlando.
          En quien estaba esperando,
          niega con mayor porfía.
               Dejaldos; que estoy cansado.
FRO.:   ¡Oh, Mengo, bien te haga Dios!
          Temor que tuve de dos,
          el tuyo me le ha quitado.

          Salen, con MENGO, BARRILDO *y el* REGIDOR.

BAR.:   ¡Vítor, Mengo!
REG.:   Y con razón.
BAR.:   ¡Mengo, vítor!
FRO.:   Eso digo.
MEN.:   ¡Ay, ay!
BAR.:   Toma, bebe, amigo.
          Come.
MEN.:   ¡Ay, ay! ¿Qué es?
BAR.:   Diacitrón.
MEN.:   ¡Ay, ay!
FRO.:   Echa de beber.
BAR.:   . . . Ya va.
FRO.:   Bien lo cuela. Bueno está.
LAU.:   Dale otra vez a comer.
MEN.:   ¡Ay, ay!
BAR.:   Esta va por mí.
LAU.:   Solenemente lo embebe.
FRO.:   El que bien niega, bien bebe.
BAR.:   ¿Quieres otra?
MEN.:   ¡Ay, ay! Sí, sí.
FRO.:   Bebe, que bien lo mereces.

JUD.:	Rest your shoulder on the board of the rack.[40]
MEN.:	Relax, and I'll tell you.
JUD.:	Who killed him?
MEN.:	Sir, Fuenteovejuna.
JUD.:	Is such roguery possible? They're laughing at the pain. The man I was expecting would talk refuses with the greatest perseverance of all. Let them go; I'm tired out.
FRO.:	Oh, Mengo, God bless you! The fear I had on your account[41] has relieved me of the fear I felt for two people.[42]

People enter, including MENGO, BARRILDO, *and the* COUNCILMAN.

BAR.:	Hurrah, Mengo!
COU.:	And rightly so.
BAR.:	Mengo, hurrah!
FRO.:	That's what *I* say.
MEN.:	Oh! Oh!
BAR.:	Take this, friend, and drink.
	Eat
MEN.:	Oh! Oh! What is it?
BAR.:	Citron preserves.
MEN.:	Oh! Oh!
FRO.:	Take a drink.
BAR.:	. . . All right now.
FRO ·	He's gulping it with a will. He's feeling fine.
LAU.:	Give him some more to eat.
MEN.:	Oh! Oh!
BAR.:	Drink this one for me.
LAU.:	He's soaking it up like nobody's business.
FRO.:	He who refuses well, drinks well.
BAR.:	Do you want another?
MEN.:	Oh! Oh! Yes, yes.
FRO.:	Drink, because you richly deserve it.

---

40. Other interpretations of this speech involve giving more pain to Mengo at this point, which doesn't seem convincing.   41. Or: "the fear you felt."   42. Probably himself and Laurencia.

LAU.:   A vez por vuelta las cuela.
FRO.:   Arrópale, que se hiela.
BAR.:   ¿Quieres más?
MEN.:   Sí, otras tres veces.
          ¡Ay, ay!
FRO.:   Si hay vino pregunta.
BAR.:   Sí hay: bebe a tu placer;
          que quien niega ha de beber.
          ¿Qué tiene?
MEN.:   Una cierta punta.
          Vamos; que me arromadizo.
FRO.:   Que lea que éste es mejor.
          ¿Quièn mató al comendador?
MEN.:   Fuenteovejunica lo hizo.

                         Vanse.

FRO.:   Justo es que honores le den.
          Pero, decidme, mi amor,
          ¿quién mató al comendador?
LAU.:   Fuenteovejuna, mi bien.
FRO.:   ¿Quién le mató?
LAU.:   ¡Dasme espanto!
          Pues Fuenteovejuna fue.
FRO.:   Y yo, ¿con qué te maté?
LAU.:   ¿Con qué? Con quererte tanto.

Vanse, y salen el REY *y la* REINA [ISABEL] *y* MANRIQUE.

ISA.:   No entendí, señor, hallaros
          aquí, y es buena mi suerte.
REY: En nueva gloria convierte
          mi vista el bien de miraros.
             Iba a Portugal de paso,
          y llegar aquí fue fuerza.
ISA.:   Vuestra majestad le tuerza
          siendo conveniente el caso.

LAU.:	He's imbibing one glass for each tug on the rack.
FRO.:	Cover him up, because he's cold.
BAR.:	Want more?
MEN.:	Yes, three more rounds.
	Oh! Oh!
FRO.:	He's asking whether there's wine.[43]
BAR.:	There is: drink as much as you like;
	because he who refuses gets to drink.
	What's wrong with it?
MEN.:	It's a little sour.
	Let's go, because I'm catching a cold.
FRO.:	Let him read that this wine is better.[44]
	Who killed the Commander?
MEN.:	Fuenteovejuna did it.

Exit [all but FRONDOSO *and* LAURENCIA].

FRO.:	It's only fair that he be honored.
	But tell me, my love,
	who killed the Commander?
LAU.:	Fuenteovejuna, darling.
FRO.:	Who killed him?
LAU.:	You're frightening me!
	I tell you, it was Fuenteovejuna.
FRO.:	And I—with what did I kill you?
LAU.:	With what? By making me love you so.

Exit. Enter the KING, QUEEN ISABEL, *and [later]* MANRIQUE.

ISA..	Sire, I didn't expect to find you
	here, and my luck is good.
KING:	The happiness of beholding you transforms
	my sight into new glory.
	I was on my way to Portugal,
	and I had to pass through here.
ISA.:	Let Your Majesty deflect your route,
	since the situation calls for it.

---

43. A very mild pun in the Spanish: Frondoso pretends to understand Mengo's lament *¡Ay!* as being *¿Hay?* ("is there any . . ."). 44. Some Spanish editors read *vea* or *beba* instead of *lea* ("let him see" or "let him drink [because]"), while others amend the line more drastically: "It's better for him to go to bed."

REY: ¿Cómo dejáis a Castilla?
ISA.:   En paz queda, quieta y llana.
REY: Siendo vos la que la allana,
          no lo tengo a maravilla.

          Sale DON MANRIQUE.

MAN.:   Para ver vuestra presencia
          el maestre de Calatrava,
          que aquí de llegar acaba,
          pide que le deis licencia,
ISA.:   Verle tenía deseado.
MAN.:   Mi fe, señora, os empeño,
          que, aunque es en edad pequeño,
          es valeroso soldado.

          Sale el MAESTRE.

MAE.:   Rodrigo Téllez Girón,
          que de loaros no acaba,
          maestre de Calatrava,
          os pide, humilde, perdón.
          Confieso que fui engañado,
          y que excedí de lo justo
          en cosas de vuestro gusto,
          como mal aconsejado.
          El consejo de Fernando
          y el interés me engañó,
          injusto fiel; y ansí yo
          perdón, humilde, os demando.
          Y si recebir merezco
          esta merced que suplico,
          desde aquí me certifico
          en que a serviros me ofrezco:
          y que en aquesta jornada
          de Granada, adonde vais,
          os prometo que veáis
          el valor que hay en mi espada;

KING: In what condition did you leave Castile?
ISA.:   It is in peace, calm and smooth.
KING: Since you were the one who smoothed it,
            I'm not at all surprised.

Enter DON MANRIQUE.

MAN.:   The Master of Calatrava,
            who has just arrived here,
            asks you to give him permission
            to enter your presence.
ISA.:   I wanted very much to see him.
MAN.:   By my faith, my lady, I assure you
            that, though young,
            he is a valiant soldier.   [*Exit.*]

Enter the MASTER.

MAS.:   I, Rodrigo Téllez Girón,
            Master of Calatrava,
            who never ceases praising you,
            humbly ask your forgiveness.
                I confess that I was misled,
            and that I exceeded proper bounds
            in matters affecting your pleasure,
            having been badly advised.
                Fernán Gómez's advice
            and personal interest misled me—
            an unjust pointer of the scales—[45]and thus I
            humbly beg your pardon.
                And if I deserve to receive
            the favor I beseech you for,
            from now on I guarantee
            that I offer myself to your service:
                and, in this campaign
            against Granada, to which you are bound,
            I promise you shall see
            the merit that lies in my sword;[46]

---

45. Or: "unjust though loyal."   46. The Catholic Monarchs didn't attack Granada until some years later, but the Master of Calatrava did join them and was killed in the fighting.

            donde sacándola apenas,
            dándoles fieras congojas,
            plantaré mis cruces rojas
            sobre sus altas almenas;
              y más, quinientos soldados
            en serviros emplearé,
            junto con la firma y fe
            de en mi vida disgustaros.
REY: Alzad, maestre, del suelo;
            que siempre que hayáis venido,
            seréis muy bien recebido.
MAE.:   Sois de afligidos consuelo.
ISA.:   Vos, con valor peregrino,
            sabéis bien decir y hacer.
MAE.:   Vos sois una bella Ester,
            y vos un Jerjes divino.

                    Sale MANRIQUE.

MAN.:   Señor, el pesquisidor
            que a Fuenteovejuna ha ido,
            con el despacho ha venido
            a verse ante tu valor.
REY: Sed juez de estos agresores.
MAE.:   Si a vos, señor, no mirara,
            sin duda les enseñara
            a matar comendadores.
REY: Eso ya no os toca a vos.
ISA.:   Yo confieso que he de ver
            el cargo en vuestro poder,
            si me lo concede Dios.

                    Sale el JUEZ.

JUEZ: A Fuenteovejuna fui
            de la suerte que has mandado,
            y con especial cuidado
            y diligencia asistí:
              haciendo averiguación

the moment I draw it there,
giving the Moors severe distress,
I shall plant my red-Cross banners
atop their lofty battlements;
    moreover, I shall employ
five hundred soldiers in your service,
together with the loyal pledge
never to give you vexation as long as I live.

KING: Master, rise from the floor;
            for, as often as you come,
            you will be very welcome.
MAS.:   You are the consolation of the afflicted.
ISA.:   With your exceptional merit,
            you speak as nobly as you act.
MAS.:   You are a beautiful Esther;
            and you, a divine Ahasuerus.

Enter MANRIQUE.

MAN.:   Sire, the investigator
            who went to Fuenteovejuna
            has arrived with his report
            for an audience with Your Majesty.
KING: Sit in judgment on these aggressors.
MAS.:   If I did not see *you* here, sire,
            I would certainly teach them
            what it means to kill Commanders.
KING: That is not a duty of yours.
ISA.:   I confess that I shall see
            the charge[47] in your hands,
            if God grants my wish.

Enter the JUDGE.

JUD.:   I went to Fuenteovejuna
            as you ordered,
            and I proceeded with special care
            and diligence;
                but after inquiring into

_____

47. The punishment of the killers? The commandery?

del cometido delito,
una hoja no se ha escrito
que sea en comprobación;
   porque conformes a una,
con un valeroso pecho,
en pidiendo quién lo ha hecho,
responden: «Fuenteovejuna».
   Trecientos he atormentado
con no pequeño rigor,
y te prometo, señor,
que más que esto no he sacado.
   Hasta niños de diez años
al potro arrimé, y no ha sido
posible haberlo inquirido
ni por halagos ni engaños.
   Y pues tan mal se acomoda
el poderlo averiguar,
a los has de perdonar,
o matar la villa toda.
   Todos vienen ante ti
para más certificarte.
de ellos podrás informarte.

REY: Que entren, pues vienen, les di.

Salen los dos ALCALDES, FRONDOSO, *las mujeres
y los villanos que quisieren.*

LAU.:   ¿Aquestos los reyes son?
FRO.:   Y en Castilla poderosos.
LAU.:   Por mi fe, que son hermosos:
   ¡bendígalos san Antón!
ISA.:   ¿Los agresores son estos?
EST.:   Fuenteovejuna, señora,
   que humildes llegan agora
   para serviros dispuestos.
     La sobrada tiranía
   y el insufrible rigor
   del muerto comendador,
   que mil insultos hacía,
     fue el autor de tanto daño.
   Las haciendas nos robaba

the crime that had been committed,
there's not a single sheet in writing
to prove any specific guilt.
   because, in total conformity,
with valiant hearts,
when I asked who had done it,
they replied: "Fuenteovejuna."
   I tortured three hundred
with no little severity,
and I assure you, sire,
that I got no more than that out of them.
   I placed even ten-year-old children
on the rack, but it wasn't
possible to learn the truth
either by cajolery or by trickery.
   And, since the possibility
of proving anything is so remote,
you've either got to pardon them
or wipe out the whole town.
   They have all come to see you
to give you stronger confirmation of this:
you can ask them yourself.

KING: Since they are here, tell them to come in.

Enter the two Mayors, FRONDOSO, the women,
and as many peasants as are wanted.

LAU.:   Is that the King and Queen?
FRO.:   Yes, and they wield great might in Castile.
LAU.:   By my faith, they're good looking;
     may Saint Anthony bless them!
ISA.:   Are these the aggressors?
EST.:   My lady, we are Fuenteovejuna,
now coming humbly
with a will to serve you.
   The excessive tyranny
and unbearable severity
of the late Commander,
who outraged us in a thousand ways,
   caused all this damage.
He stole our property

y las doncellas forzaba,
siendo de piedad extraño.

FRO.: Tanto, que aquesta zagala,
que el cielo me ha concedido,
en que tan dichoso he sido
que nadie en dicha me iguala,
  cuando conmigo casó,
aquella noche primera,
mejor que si suya fuera,
a su casa la llevó;
  y a no saberse guardar
ella, que en virtud florece,
ya manifesto parece
lo que pudiera pasar.

MEN.: ¿No es ya tiempo que hable yo?
Si me dais licencia, entiendo
que os admiraréis, sabiendo
del modo que me trató.
  Porque quise defender
una moza de su gente,
que con término insolente
fuerza la querían hacer,
  aquel perverso Nerón,
de manera me ha tratado,
que el reverso me ha dejado
como rueda de salmón.
  Tocaron mis atabales
tres hombres con tal porfía,
que aun pienso que todavía
me duran los cardenales.
  Gasté en este mal prolijo,
por que el cuero se me curta,
polvos de arrayán y murta
más que vale mi cortijo.

EST.: Señor, tuyos ser queremos.
Rey nuestro eres natural,
y con título de tal
ya tus armas puesto habemos.
  Esperamos tu clemencia,
y que veas, esperamos,
que en este caso te damos

[handwritten: Hay clemencia]

[handwritten: expresar poder collectivo]

and raped our young women,
a stranger to mercy.

FRO.:   So much so, that this girl,
whom heaven has granted to me,
making me so fortunate
that nobody's good fortune is equal to mine,
   when she married me,
on that first night,
just as if she belonged to him,
he carried her off to his house;
   and, if she hadn't known how to protect
herself, and been such a blossom of virtue,
it's all too clear
what might have happened.

MEN.:   Isn't it time for me to speak?
If you give me leave, I expect
that you'll be astounded to learn
the way he treated me.
   Because I tried to defend
a girl from his people,
who were insolently
trying to abduct her,
   that cruel Nero
treated me in such a way
that he left my behind
looking like a slice of salmon.
   Three men assailed
my backside so persistently
that I even think the welts
will last forever.
   On this protracted malady,
in order for my hide to be made whole,
I've spent more on myrtle powder and berries
than my whole farm is worth.

EST.:   Sire, we wish to belong to you.
You are our natural king,
and, naming you as such,
we have already installed your coat-of-arms.
   We hope for your clemency,
and we hope you will see
that in this situation we are offering you

por abono la inocencia.

REY:
Pues no puede averiguarse
el suceso por escrito,
aunque fue grave el delito,
por fuerza ha de perdonarse.
Y la villa es bien se quede
en mí, pues de mí se vale,
hasta ver si acaso sale
comendador que la herede.

FRO.:
Su majestad habla, en fin,
como quien tanto ha acertado.
Y aquí, discreto senado,
Fuenteovejuna da fin.

[marginal handwritten note: No castiga el pueblo... él entiende]

our innocence as security.

KING: Since the incident cannot
be proved in writing,
even though the crime was serious, *differs from the chronicle*
it has to be forgiven.
    And it's a good thing for the town
to remain mine, since it claims my protection,
until we see whether by chance
another Commander is appointed to inherit it.

FRO.:   In short, Your Majesty speaks
like a man who has been right in so many matters.
And here, wise spectators,
Fuenteovejuna comes to an end.

A CATALOG OF SELECTED
DOVER BOOKS
IN ALL FIELDS OF INTEREST

A CATALOG OF SELECTED DOVER BOOKS IN ALL FIELDS OF INTEREST

100 BEST-LOVED POEMS, Edited by Philip Smith. "The Passionate Shepherd to His Love," "Shall I compare thee to a summer's day?" "Death, be not proud," "The Raven," "The Road Not Taken," plus works by Blake, Wordsworth, Byron, Shelley, Keats, many others. 96pp. 5³⁄₁₆ x 8¼. 0-486-28553-7

100 SMALL HOUSES OF THE THIRTIES, Brown-Blodgett Company. Exterior photographs and floor plans for 100 charming structures. Illustrations of models accompanied by descriptions of interiors, color schemes, closet space, and other amenities. 200 illustrations. 112pp. 8⅜ x 11. 0-486-44131-8

1000 TURN-OF-THE-CENTURY HOUSES: With Illustrations and Floor Plans, Herbert C. Chivers. Reproduced from a rare edition, this showcase of homes ranges from cottages and bungalows to sprawling mansions. Each house is meticulously illustrated and accompanied by complete floor plans. 256pp. 9⅜ x 12¼. 0-486-45596-3

101 GREAT AMERICAN POEMS, Edited by The American Poetry & Literacy Project. Rich treasury of verse from the 19th and 20th centuries includes works by Edgar Allan Poe, Robert Frost, Walt Whitman, Langston Hughes, Emily Dickinson, T. S. Eliot, other notables. 96pp. 5³⁄₁₆ x 8¼. 0-486-40158-8

101 GREAT SAMURAI PRINTS, Utagawa Kuniyoshi. Kuniyoshi was a master of the warrior woodblock print — and these 18th-century illustrations represent the pinnacle of his craft. Full-color portraits of renowned Japanese samurais pulse with movement, passion, and remarkably fine detail. 112pp. 8⅜ x 11. 0-486-46523-3

ABC OF BALLET, Janet Grosser. Clearly worded, abundantly illustrated little guide defines basic ballet-related terms: arabesque, battement, pas de chat, relevé, sissonne, many others. Pronunciation guide included. Excellent primer. 48pp. 4³⁄₁₆ x 5¾. 0-486-40871-X

ACCESSORIES OF DRESS: An Illustrated Encyclopedia, Katherine Lester and Bess Viola Oerke. Illustrations of hats, veils, wigs, cravats, shawls, shoes, gloves, and other accessories enhance an engaging commentary that reveals the humor and charm of the many-sided story of accessorized apparel. 644 figures and 59 plates. 608pp. 6 ⅛ x 9¼. 0-486-43378-1

ADVENTURES OF HUCKLEBERRY FINN, Mark Twain. Join Huck and Jim as their boyhood adventures along the Mississippi River lead them into a world of excitement, danger, and self-discovery. Humorous narrative, lyrical descriptions of the Mississippi valley, and memorable characters. 224pp. 5³⁄₁₆ x 8¼. 0-486-28061-6

ALICE STARMORE'S BOOK OF FAIR ISLE KNITTING, Alice Starmore. A noted designer from the region of Scotland's Fair Isle explores the history and techniques of this distinctive, stranded-color knitting style and provides copious illustrated instructions for 14 original knitwear designs. 208pp. 8⅜ x 10⅞. 0-486-47218-3

Browse over 9,000 books at www.doverpublications.com

ALICE'S ADVENTURES IN WONDERLAND, Lewis Carroll. Beloved classic about a little girl lost in a topsy-turvy land and her encounters with the White Rabbit, March Hare, Mad Hatter, Cheshire Cat, and other delightfully improbable characters. 42 illustrations by Sir John Tenniel. 96pp. 5³⁄₁₆ x 8¼. 0-486-27543-4

AMERICA'S LIGHTHOUSES: An Illustrated History, Francis Ross Holland. Profusely illustrated fact-filled survey of American lighthouses since 1716. Over 200 stations — East, Gulf, and West coasts, Great Lakes, Hawaii, Alaska, Puerto Rico, the Virgin Islands, and the Mississippi and St. Lawrence Rivers. 240pp. 8 x 10¾. 0-486-25576-X

AN ENCYCLOPEDIA OF THE VIOLIN, Alberto Bachmann. Translated by Frederick H. Martens. Introduction by Eugene Ysaye. First published in 1925, this renowned reference remains unsurpassed as a source of essential information, from construction and evolution to repertoire and technique. Includes a glossary and 73 illustrations. 496pp. 6⅛ x 9¼. 0-486-46618-3

ANIMALS: 1,419 Copyright-Free Illustrations of Mammals, Birds, Fish, Insects, etc., Selected by Jim Harter. Selected for its visual impact and ease of use, this outstanding collection of wood engravings presents over 1,000 species of animals in extremely lifelike poses. Includes mammals, birds, reptiles, amphibians, fish, insects, and other invertebrates. 284pp. 9 x 12. 0-486-23766-4

THE ANNALS, Tacitus. Translated by Alfred John Church and William Jackson Brodribb. This vital chronicle of Imperial Rome, written by the era's great historian, spans A.D. 14-68 and paints incisive psychological portraits of major figures, from Tiberius to Nero. 416pp. 5³⁄₁₆ x 8¼. 0-486-45236-0

ANTIGONE, Sophocles. Filled with passionate speeches and sensitive probing of moral and philosophical issues, this powerful and often-performed Greek drama reveals the grim fate that befalls the children of Oedipus. Footnotes. 64pp. 5³⁄₁₆ x 8 ¼. 0-486-27804-2

ART DECO DECORATIVE PATTERNS IN FULL COLOR, Christian Stoll. Reprinted from a rare 1910 portfolio, 160 sensuous and exotic images depict a breathtaking array of florals, geometrics, and abstracts — all elegant in their stark simplicity. 64pp. 8⅜ x 11. 0-486-44862-2

THE ARTHUR RACKHAM TREASURY: 86 Full-Color Illustrations, Arthur Rackham. Selected and Edited by Jeff A. Menges. A stunning treasury of 86 full-page plates span the famed English artist's career, from Rip Van Winkle (1905) to masterworks such as Undine, A Midsummer Night's Dream, and Wind in the Willows (1939). 96pp. 8⅜ x 11 0-486-44685-9

THE AUTHENTIC GILBERT & SULLIVAN SONGBOOK, W. S. Gilbert and A. S. Sullivan. The most comprehensive collection available, this songbook includes selections from every one of Gilbert and Sullivan's light operas. Ninety-two numbers are presented uncut and unedited, and in their original keys. 410pp. 9 x 12. 0-486-23482-7

THE AWAKENING, Kate Chopin. First published in 1899, this controversial novel of a New Orleans wife's search for love outside a stifling marriage shocked readers. Today, it remains a first-rate narrative with superb characterization. New introductory Note. 128pp. 5³⁄₁₆ x 8¼. 0-486-27786-0

BASIC DRAWING, Louis Priscilla. Beginning with perspective, this commonsense manual progresses to the figure in movement, light and shade, anatomy, drapery, composition, trees and landscape, and outdoor sketching. Black-and-white illustrations throughout. 128pp. 8⅜ x 11. 0-486-45815-6

Browse over 9,000 books at www.doverpublications.com

THE BATTLES THAT CHANGED HISTORY, Fletcher Pratt. Historian profiles 16 crucial conflicts, ancient to modern, that changed the course of Western civilization. Gripping accounts of battles led by Alexander the Great, Joan of Arc, Ulysses S. Grant, other commanders. 27 maps. 352pp. 5⅜ x 8½.   0-486-41129-X

BEETHOVEN'S LETTERS, Ludwig van Beethoven. Edited by Dr. A. C. Kalischer. Features 457 letters to fellow musicians, friends, greats, patrons, and literary men. Reveals musical thoughts, quirks of personality, insights, and daily events. Includes 15 plates. 410pp. 5⅜ x 8½.   0-486-22769-3

BERNICE BOBS HER HAIR AND OTHER STORIES, F. Scott Fitzgerald. This brilliant anthology includes 6 of Fitzgerald's most popular stories: "The Diamond as Big as the Ritz," the title tale, "The Offshore Pirate," "The Ice Palace," "The Jelly Bean," and "May Day." 176pp. 5⅜ x 8½.   0-486-47049-0

BESLER'S BOOK OF FLOWERS AND PLANTS: 73 Full-Color Plates from Hortus Eystettensis, 1613, Basilius Besler. Here is a selection of magnificent plates from the *Hortus Eystettensis*, which vividly illustrated and identified the plants, flowers, and trees that thrived in the legendary German garden at Eichstätt. 80pp. 8⅜ x 11.
            0-486-46005-3

THE BOOK OF KELLS, Edited by Blanche Cirker. Painstakingly reproduced from a rare facsimile edition, this volume contains full-page decorations, portraits, illustrations, plus a sampling of textual leaves with exquisite calligraphy and ornamentation. 32 full-color illustrations. 32pp. 9⅜ x 12¼.   0-486-24345-1

THE BOOK OF THE CROSSBOW: With an Additional Section on Catapults and Other Siege Engines, Ralph Payne-Gallwey. Fascinating study traces history and use of crossbow as military and sporting weapon, from Middle Ages to modern times. Also covers related weapons: balistas, catapults, Turkish bows, more. Over 240 illustrations. 400pp. 7¼ x 10⅛.   0-486-28720-3

THE BUNGALOW BOOK: Floor Plans and Photos of 112 Houses, 1910, Henry L. Wilson. Here are 112 of the most popular and economic blueprints of the early 20th century — plus an illustration or photograph of each completed house. A wonderful time capsule that still offers a wealth of valuable insights. 160pp. 8⅜ x 11.
            0-486-45104-6

THE CALL OF THE WILD, Jack London. A classic novel of adventure, drawn from London's own experiences as a Klondike adventurer, relating the story of a heroic dog caught in the brutal life of the Alaska Gold Rush. Note. 64pp. 5³⁄₁₆ x 8¼.
            0-486-26472-6

CANDIDE, Voltaire. Edited by Francois-Marie Arouet. One of the world's great satires since its first publication in 1759. Witty, caustic skewering of romance, science, philosophy, religion, government — nearly all human ideals and institutions. 112pp. 5³⁄₁₆ x 8¼.   0-486-26689-3

CELEBRATED IN THEIR TIME: Photographic Portraits from the George Grantham Bain Collection, Edited by Amy Pastan. With an Introduction by Michael Carlebach. Remarkable portrait gallery features 112 rare images of Albert Einstein, Charlie Chaplin, the Wright Brothers, Henry Ford, and other luminaries from the worlds of politics, art, entertainment, and industry. 128pp. 8⅜ x 11.   0-486-46754-6

CHARIOTS FOR APOLLO: The NASA History of Manned Lunar Spacecraft to 1969, Courtney G. Brooks, James M. Grimwood, and Loyd S. Swenson, Jr. This illustrated history by a trio of experts is the definitive reference on the Apollo spacecraft and lunar modules. It traces the vehicles' design, development, and operation in space. More than 100 photographs and illustrations. 576pp. 6¾ x 9¼. 0-486-46756-2

Browse over 9,000 books at www.doverpublications.com

A CHRISTMAS CAROL, Charles Dickens. This engrossing tale relates Ebenezer Scrooge's ghostly journeys through Christmases past, present, and future and his ultimate transformation from a harsh and grasping old miser to a charitable and compassionate human being. 80pp. 5$\frac{3}{16}$ x 8$\frac{1}{4}$. 0-486-26865-9

COMMON SENSE, Thomas Paine. First published in January of 1776, this highly influential landmark document clearly and persuasively argued for American separation from Great Britain and paved the way for the Declaration of Independence. 64pp. 5$\frac{3}{16}$ x 8$\frac{1}{4}$. 0-486-29602-4

THE COMPLETE SHORT STORIES OF OSCAR WILDE, Oscar Wilde. Complete texts of "The Happy Prince and Other Tales," "A House of Pomegranates," "Lord Arthur Savile's Crime and Other Stories," "Poems in Prose," and "The Portrait of Mr. W. H." 208pp. 5$\frac{3}{16}$ x 8$\frac{1}{4}$. 0-486-45216-6

COMPLETE SONNETS, William Shakespeare. Over 150 exquisite poems deal with love, friendship, the tyranny of time, beauty's evanescence, death, and other themes in language of remarkable power, precision, and beauty. Glossary of archaic terms. 80pp. 5$\frac{3}{16}$ x 8$\frac{1}{4}$. 0-486-26686-9

THE COUNT OF MONTE CRISTO: Abridged Edition, Alexandre Dumas. Falsely accused of treason, Edmond Dantès is imprisoned in the bleak Chateau d'If. After a hair-raising escape, he launches an elaborate plot to extract a bitter revenge against those who betrayed him. 448pp. 5$\frac{3}{16}$ x 8$\frac{1}{4}$. 0-486-45643-9

CRAFTSMAN BUNGALOWS: Designs from the Pacific Northwest, Yoho & Merritt. This reprint of a rare catalog, showcasing the charming simplicity and cozy style of Craftsman bungalows, is filled with photos of completed homes, plus floor plans and estimated costs. An indispensable resource for architects, historians, and illustrators. 112pp. 10 x 7. 0-486-46875-5

CRAFTSMAN BUNGALOWS: 59 Homes from "The Craftsman," Edited by Gustav Stickley. Best and most attractive designs from Arts and Crafts Movement publication — 1903–1916 — includes sketches, photographs of homes, floor plans, descriptive text. 128pp. 8$\frac{1}{4}$ x 11. 0-486-25829-7

CRIME AND PUNISHMENT, Fyodor Dostoyevsky. Translated by Constance Garnett. Supreme masterpiece tells the story of Raskolnikov, a student tormented by his own thoughts after he murders an old woman. Overwhelmed by guilt and terror, he confesses and goes to prison. 480pp. 5$\frac{3}{16}$ x 8$\frac{1}{4}$. 0-486-41587-2

THE DECLARATION OF INDEPENDENCE AND OTHER GREAT DOCUMENTS OF AMERICAN HISTORY, 1775-1865, Edited by John Grafton. Thirteen compelling and influential documents: Henry's "Give Me Liberty or Give Me Death," Declaration of Independence, The Constitution, Washington's First Inaugural Address, The Monroe Doctrine, The Emancipation Proclamation, Gettysburg Address, more. 64pp. 5$\frac{3}{16}$ x 8$\frac{1}{4}$. 0-486-41124-9

THE DESERT AND THE SOWN: Travels in Palestine and Syria, Gertrude Bell. "The female Lawrence of Arabia," Gertrude Bell wrote captivating, perceptive accounts of her travels in the Middle East. This intriguing narrative, accompanied by 160 photos, traces her 1905 sojourn in Lebanon, Syria, and Palestine. 368pp. 5$\frac{3}{8}$ x 8$\frac{1}{2}$. 0-486-46876-3

A DOLL'S HOUSE, Henrik Ibsen. Ibsen's best-known play displays his genius for realistic prose drama. An expression of women's rights, the play climaxes when the central character, Nora, rejects a smothering marriage and life in "a doll's house." 80pp. 5$\frac{3}{16}$ x 8$\frac{1}{4}$. 0-486-27062-9

Browse over 9,000 books at www.doverpublications.com

DOOMED SHIPS: Great Ocean Liner Disasters, William H. Miller, Jr. Nearly 200 photographs, many from private collections, highlight tales of some of the vessels whose pleasure cruises ended in catastrophe: the *Morro Castle, Normandie, Andrea Doria, Europa,* and many others. 128pp. 8⅞ x 11¼. 0-486-45366-9

THE DORÉ BIBLE ILLUSTRATIONS, Gustave Doré. Detailed plates from the Bible: the Creation scenes, Adam and Eve, horrifying visions of the Flood, the battle sequences with their monumental crowds, depictions of the life of Jesus, 241 plates in all. 241pp. 9 x 12. 0-486-23004-X

DRAWING DRAPERY FROM HEAD TO TOE, Cliff Young. Expert guidance on how to draw shirts, pants, skirts, gloves, hats, and coats on the human figure, including folds in relation to the body, pull and crush, action folds, creases, more. Over 200 drawings. 48pp. 8¼ x 11. 0-486-45591-2

DUBLINERS, James Joyce. A fine and accessible introduction to the work of one of the 20th century's most influential writers, this collection features 15 tales, including a masterpiece of the short-story genre, "The Dead." 160pp. 5³⁄₁₆ x 8¼. 0-486-26870-5

EASY-TO-MAKE POP-UPS, Joan Irvine. Illustrated by Barbara Reid. Dozens of wonderful ideas for three-dimensional paper fun — from holiday greeting cards with moving parts to a pop-up menagerie. Easy-to-follow, illustrated instructions for more than 30 projects. 299 black-and-white illustrations. 96pp. 8⅜ x 11. 0-486-44622-0

EASY-TO-MAKE STORYBOOK DOLLS: A "Novel" Approach to Cloth Dollmaking, Sherralyn St. Clair. Favorite fictional characters come alive in this unique beginner's dollmaking guide. Includes patterns for Pollyanna, Dorothy from *The Wonderful Wizard of Oz,* Mary of *The Secret Garden,* plus easy-to-follow instructions, 263 black-and-white illustrations, and an 8-page color insert. 112pp. 8¼ x 11. 0-486-47360-0

EINSTEIN'S ESSAYS IN SCIENCE, Albert Einstein. Speeches and essays in accessible, everyday language profile influential physicists such as Niels Bohr and Isaac Newton. They also explore areas of physics to which the author made major contributions. 128pp. 5 x 8. 0-486-47011-3

EL DORADO: Further Adventures of the Scarlet Pimpernel, Baroness Orczy. A popular sequel to *The Scarlet Pimpernel,* this suspenseful story recounts the Pimpernel's attempts to rescue the Dauphin from imprisonment during the French Revolution. An irresistible blend of intrigue, period detail, and vibrant characterizations. 352pp. 5³⁄₁₆ x 8¼. 0-486-44026-5

ELEGANT SMALL HOMES OF THE TWENTIES: 99 Designs from a Competition, Chicago Tribune. Nearly 100 designs for five- and six-room houses feature New England and Southern colonials, Normandy cottages, stately Italianate dwellings, and other fascinating snapshots of American domestic architecture of the 1920s. 112pp. 9 x 12. 0-486-46910-7

THE ELEMENTS OF STYLE: The Original Edition, William Strunk, Jr. This is the book that generations of writers have relied upon for timeless advice on grammar, diction, syntax, and other essentials. In concise terms, it identifies the principal requirements of proper style and common errors. 64pp. 5⅜ x 8½. 0-486-44798-7

THE ELUSIVE PIMPERNEL, Baroness Orczy. Robespierre's revolutionaries find their wicked schemes thwarted by the heroic Pimpernel — Sir Percival Blakeney. In this thrilling sequel, Chauvelin devises a plot to eliminate the Pimpernel and his wife. 272pp. 5³⁄₁₆ x 8¼. 0-486-45464-9

Browse over 9,000 books at www.doverpublications.com

AN ENCYCLOPEDIA OF BATTLES: Accounts of Over 1,560 Battles from 1479 B.C. to the Present, David Eggenberger. Essential details of every major battle in recorded history from the first battle of Megiddo in 1479 B.C. to Grenada in 1984. List of battle maps. 99 illustrations. 544pp. 6½ x 9¼. 0-486-24913-1

ENCYCLOPEDIA OF EMBROIDERY STITCHES, INCLUDING CREWEL, Marion Nichols. Precise explanations and instructions, clearly illustrated, on how to work chain, back, cross, knotted, woven stitches, and many more — 178 in all, including Cable Outline, Whipped Satin, and Eyelet Buttonhole. Over 1400 illustrations. 219pp. 8⅜ x 11¼. 0-486-22929-7

ENTER JEEVES: 15 Early Stories, P. G. Wodehouse. Splendid collection contains first 8 stories featuring Bertie Wooster, the deliciously dim aristocrat and Jeeves, his brainy, imperturbable manservant. Also, the complete Reggie Pepper (Bertie's prototype) series. 288pp. 5⅜ x 8½. 0-486-29717-9

ERIC SLOANE'S AMERICA: Paintings in Oil, Michael Wigley. With a Foreword by Mimi Sloane. Eric Sloane's evocative oils of America's landscape and material culture shimmer with immense historical and nostalgic appeal. This original hardcover collection gathers nearly a hundred of his finest paintings, with subjects ranging from New England to the American Southwest. 128pp. 10⅝ x 9. 0-486-46525-X

ETHAN FROME, Edith Wharton. Classic story of wasted lives, set against a bleak New England background. Superbly delineated characters in a hauntingly grim tale of thwarted love. Considered by many to be Wharton's masterpiece. 96pp. 5$^{3}/_{16}$ x 8 ¼. 0-486-26690-7

THE EVERLASTING MAN, G. K. Chesterton. Chesterton's view of Christianity — as a blend of philosophy and mythology, satisfying intellect and spirit — applies to his brilliant book, which appeals to readers' heads as well as their hearts. 288pp. 5⅜ x 8½. 0-486-46036-3

THE FIELD AND FOREST HANDY BOOK, Daniel Beard. Written by a co-founder of the Boy Scouts, this appealing guide offers illustrated instructions for building kites, birdhouses, boats, igloos, and other fun projects, plus numerous helpful tips for campers. 448pp. 5$^{3}/_{16}$ x 8¼. 0-486-46191-2

FINDING YOUR WAY WITHOUT MAP OR COMPASS, Harold Gatty. Useful, instructive manual shows would-be explorers, hikers, bikers, scouts, sailors, and survivalists how to find their way outdoors by observing animals, weather patterns, shifting sands, and other elements of nature. 288pp. 5⅜ x 8½. 0-486-40613-X

FIRST FRENCH READER: A Beginner's Dual-Language Book, Edited and Translated by Stanley Appelbaum. This anthology introduces 50 legendary writers — Voltaire, Balzac, Baudelaire, Proust, more — through passages from *The Red and the Black, Les Misérables, Madame Bovary,* and other classics. Original French text plus English translation on facing pages. 240pp. 5⅜ x 8½. 0-486-46178-5

FIRST GERMAN READER: A Beginner's Dual-Language Book, Edited by Harry Steinhauer. Specially chosen for their power to evoke German life and culture, these short, simple readings include poems, stories, essays, and anecdotes by Goethe, Hesse, Heine, Schiller, and others. 224pp. 5⅜ x 8½. 0-486-46179-3

FIRST SPANISH READER: A Beginner's Dual-Language Book, Angel Flores. Delightful stories, other material based on works of Don Juan Manuel, Luis Taboada, Ricardo Palma, other noted writers. Complete faithful English translations on facing pages. Exercises. 176pp. 5⅜ x 8½. 0-486-25810-6

Browse over 9,000 books at www.doverpublications.com

FIVE ACRES AND INDEPENDENCE, Maurice G. Kains. Great back-to-the-land classic explains basics of self-sufficient farming. The one book to get. 95 illustrations. 397pp. 5⅜ x 8½. 0-486-20974-1

FLAGG'S SMALL HOUSES: Their Economic Design and Construction, 1922, Ernest Flagg. Although most famous for his skyscrapers, Flagg was also a proponent of the well-designed single-family dwelling. His classic treatise features innovations that save space, materials, and cost. 526 illustrations. 160pp. 9⅜ x 12¼. 0-486-45197-6

FLATLAND: A Romance of Many Dimensions, Edwin A. Abbott. Classic of science (and mathematical) fiction — charmingly illustrated by the author — describes the adventures of A. Square, a resident of Flatland, in Spaceland (three dimensions), Lineland (one dimension), and Pointland (no dimensions). 96pp. 5³⁄₁₆ x 8¼. 0-486-27263-X

FRANKENSTEIN, Mary Shelley. The story of Victor Frankenstein's monstrous creation and the havoc it caused has enthralled generations of readers and inspired countless writers of horror and suspense. With the author's own 1831 introduction. 176pp. 5³⁄₁₆ x 8¼. 0-486-28211-2

THE GARGOYLE BOOK: 572 Examples from Gothic Architecture, Lester Burbank Bridaham. Dispelling the conventional wisdom that French Gothic architectural flourishes were born of despair or gloom, Bridaham reveals the whimsical nature of these creations and the ingenious artisans who made them. 572 illustrations. 224pp. 8⅜ x 11. 0-486-44754-5

THE GIFT OF THE MAGI AND OTHER SHORT STORIES, O. Henry. Sixteen captivating stories by one of America's most popular storytellers. Included are such classics as "The Gift of the Magi," "The Last Leaf," and "The Ransom of Red Chief." Publisher's Note. 96pp. 5³⁄₁₆ x 8¼. 0-486-27061-0

THE GOETHE TREASURY: Selected Prose and Poetry, Johann Wolfgang von Goethe. Edited, Selected, and with an Introduction by Thomas Mann. In addition to his lyric poetry, Goethe wrote travel sketches, autobiographical studies, essays, letters, and proverbs in rhyme and prose. This collection presents outstanding examples from each genre. 368pp. 5⅜ x 8½. 0-486-44780-4

GREAT EXPECTATIONS, Charles Dickens. Orphaned Pip is apprenticed to the dirty work of the forge but dreams of becoming a gentleman — and one day finds himself in possession of "great expectations." Dickens' finest novel. 400pp. 5³⁄₁₆ x 8¼. 0-486-41586-4

GREAT WRITERS ON THE ART OF FICTION: From Mark Twain to Joyce Carol Oates, Edited by James Daley. An indispensable source of advice and inspiration, this anthology features essays by Henry James, Kate Chopin, Willa Cather, Sinclair Lewis, Jack London, Raymond Chandler, Raymond Carver, Eudora Welty, and Kurt Vonnegut, Jr. 192pp. 5⅜ x 8½. 0-486-45128-3

HAMLET, William Shakespeare. The quintessential Shakespearean tragedy, whose highly charged confrontations and anguished soliloquies probe depths of human feeling rarely sounded in any art. Reprinted from an authoritative British edition complete with illuminating footnotes. 128pp. 5³⁄₁₆ x 8¼. 0-486-27278-8

THE HAUNTED HOUSE, Charles Dickens. A Yuletide gathering in an eerie country retreat provides the backdrop for Dickens and his friends — including Elizabeth Gaskell and Wilkie Collins — who take turns spinning supernatural yarns. 144pp. 5⅜ x 8½. 0-486-46309-5

HEART OF DARKNESS, Joseph Conrad. Dark allegory of a journey up the Congo River and the narrator's encounter with the mysterious Mr. Kurtz. Masterly blend of adventure, character study, psychological penetration. For many, Conrad's finest, most enigmatic story. 80pp. 5³⁄₁₆ x 8¼. 0-486-26464-5

HENSON AT THE NORTH POLE, Matthew A. Henson. This thrilling memoir by the heroic African-American who was Peary's companion through two decades of Arctic exploration recounts a tale of danger, courage, and determination. "Fascinating and exciting." — *Commonweal.* 128pp. 5⅜ x 8½. 0-486-45472-X

HISTORIC COSTUMES AND HOW TO MAKE THEM, Mary Fernald and E. Shenton. Practical, informative guidebook shows how to create everything from short tunics worn by Saxon men in the fifth century to a lady's bustle dress of the late 1800s. 81 illustrations. 176pp. 5⅜ x 8½. 0-486-44906-8

THE HOUND OF THE BASKERVILLES, Arthur Conan Doyle. A deadly curse in the form of a legendary ferocious beast continues to claim its victims from the Baskerville family until Holmes and Watson intervene. Often called the best detective story ever written. 128pp. 5³⁄₁₆ x 8¼. 0-486-28214-7

THE HOUSE BEHIND THE CEDARS, Charles W. Chesnutt. Originally published in 1900, this groundbreaking novel by a distinguished African-American author recounts the drama of a brother and sister who "pass for white" during the dangerous days of Reconstruction. 208pp. 5⅜ x 8½. 0-486-46144-0

THE HUMAN FIGURE IN MOTION, Eadweard Muybridge. The 4,789 photographs in this definitive selection show the human figure — models almost all undraped — engaged in over 160 different types of action: running, climbing stairs, etc. 390pp. 7⅞ x 10⅝. 0-486-20204-6

THE IMPORTANCE OF BEING EARNEST, Oscar Wilde. Wilde's witty and buoyant comedy of manners, filled with some of literature's most famous epigrams, reprinted from an authoritative British edition. Considered Wilde's most perfect work. 64pp. 5³⁄₁₆ x 8¼. 0-486-26478-5

THE INFERNO, Dante Alighieri. Translated and with notes by Henry Wadsworth Longfellow. The first stop on Dante's famous journey from Hell to Purgatory to Paradise, this 14th-century allegorical poem blends vivid and shocking imagery with graceful lyricism. Translated by the beloved 19th-century poet, Henry Wadsworth Longfellow. 256pp. 5³⁄₁₆ x 8¼. 0-486-44288-8

JANE EYRE, Charlotte Brontë. Written in 1847, *Jane Eyre* tells the tale of an orphan girl's progress from the custody of cruel relatives to an oppressive boarding school and its culmination in a troubled career as a governess. 448pp. 5³⁄₁₆ x 8¼. 0-486-42449-9

JAPANESE WOODBLOCK FLOWER PRINTS, Tanigami Kônan. Extraordinary collection of Japanese woodblock prints by a well-known artist features 120 plates in brilliant color. Realistic images from a rare edition include daffodils, tulips, and other familiar and unusual flowers. 128pp. 11 x 8¼. 0-486-46442-3

JEWELRY MAKING AND DESIGN, Augustus F. Rose and Antonio Cirino. Professional secrets of jewelry making are revealed in a thorough, practical guide. Over 200 illustrations. 306pp. 5⅜ x 8½. 0-486-21750-7

JULIUS CAESAR, William Shakespeare. Great tragedy based on Plutarch's account of the lives of Brutus, Julius Caesar and Mark Antony. Evil plotting, ringing oratory, high tragedy with Shakespeare's incomparable insight, dramatic power. Explanatory footnotes. 96pp. 5³⁄₁₆ x 8¼. 0-486-26876-4

THE JUNGLE, Upton Sinclair. 1906 bestseller shockingly reveals intolerable labor practices and working conditions in the Chicago stockyards as it tells the grim story of a Slavic family that emigrates to America full of optimism but soon faces despair. 320pp. 5³⁄₁₆ x 8¼.   0-486-41923-1

THE KINGDOM OF GOD IS WITHIN YOU, Leo Tolstoy. The soul-searching book that inspired Gandhi to embrace the concept of passive resistance, Tolstoy's 1894 polemic clearly outlines a radical, well-reasoned revision of traditional Christian thinking. 352pp. 5³⁄₁₆ x 8¼.   0-486-45138-0

THE LADY OR THE TIGER?: and Other Logic Puzzles, Raymond M. Smullyan. Created by a renowned puzzle master, these whimsically themed challenges involve paradoxes about probability, time, and change; metapuzzles; and self-referentiality. Nineteen chapters advance in difficulty from relatively simple to highly complex. 1982 edition. 240pp. 5⅜ x 8½.   0-486-47027-X

LEAVES OF GRASS: The Original 1855 Edition, Walt Whitman. Whitman's immortal collection includes some of the greatest poems of modern times, including his masterpiece, "Song of Myself." Shattering standard conventions, it stands as an unabashed celebration of body and nature. 128pp. 5³⁄₁₆ x 8¼.   0-486-45676-5

LES MISÉRABLES, Victor Hugo. Translated by Charles E. Wilbour. Abridged by James K. Robinson. A convict's heroic struggle for justice and redemption plays out against a fiery backdrop of the Napoleonic wars. This edition features the excellent original translation and a sensitive abridgment. 304pp. 6⅛ x 9¼.
                                                                        0-486-45789-3

LILITH: A Romance, George MacDonald. In this novel by the father of fantasy literature, a man travels through time to meet Adam and Eve and to explore humanity's fall from grace and ultimate redemption. 240pp. 5⅜ x 8½.
                                                                        0-486-46818-6

THE LOST LANGUAGE OF SYMBOLISM, Harold Bayley. This remarkable book reveals the hidden meaning behind familiar images and words, from the origins of Santa Claus to the fleur-de-lys, drawing from mythology, folklore, religious texts, and fairy tales. 1,418 illustrations. 784pp. 5⅜ x 8½.   0-486-44787-1

MACBETH, William Shakespeare. A Scottish nobleman murders the king in order to succeed to the throne. Tortured by his conscience and fearful of discovery, he becomes tangled in a web of treachery and deceit that ultimately spells his doom. 96pp. 5³⁄₁₆ x 8¼.   0-486-27802-6

MAKING AUTHENTIC CRAFTSMAN FURNITURE: Instructions and Plans for 62 Projects, Gustav Stickley. Make authentic reproductions of handsome, functional, durable furniture: tables, chairs, wall cabinets, desks, a hall tree, and more. Construction plans with drawings, schematics, dimensions, and lumber specs reprinted from 1900s The Craftsman magazine. 128pp. 8⅛ x 11.   0-486-25000-8

MATHEMATICS FOR THE NONMATHEMATICIAN, Morris Kline. Erudite and entertaining overview follows development of mathematics from ancient Greeks to present. Topics include logic and mathematics, the fundamental concept, differential calculus, probability theory, much more. Exercises and problems. 641pp. 5⅜ x 8½.   0-486-24823-2

MEMOIRS OF AN ARABIAN PRINCESS FROM ZANZIBAR, Emily Ruete. This 19th-century autobiography offers a rare inside look at the society surrounding a sultan's palace. A real-life princess in exile recalls her vanished world of harems, slave trading, and court intrigues. 288pp. 5⅜ x 8½.   0-486-47121-7

THE METAMORPHOSIS AND OTHER STORIES, Franz Kafka. Excellent new English translations of title story (considered by many critics Kafka's most perfect work), plus "The Judgment," "In the Penal Colony," "A Country Doctor," and "A Report to an Academy." Note. 96pp. 5³⁄₁₆ x 8¼. 0-486-29030-1

MICROSCOPIC ART FORMS FROM THE PLANT WORLD, R. Anheisser. From undulating curves to complex geometrics, a world of fascinating images abound in this classic, illustrated survey of microscopic plants. Features 400 detailed illustrations of nature's minute but magnificent handiwork. The accompanying CD-ROM includes all of the images in the book. 128pp. 9 x 9. 0-486-46013-4

A MIDSUMMER NIGHT'S DREAM, William Shakespeare. Among the most popular of Shakespeare's comedies, this enchanting play humorously celebrates the vagaries of love as it focuses upon the intertwined romances of several pairs of lovers. Explanatory footnotes. 80pp. 5³⁄₁₆ x 8¼. 0-486-27067-X

THE MONEY CHANGERS, Upton Sinclair. Originally published in 1908, this cautionary novel from the author of *The Jungle* explores corruption within the American system as a group of power brokers joins forces for personal gain, triggering a crash on Wall Street. 192pp. 5⅜ x 8½. 0-486-46917-4

THE MOST POPULAR HOMES OF THE TWENTIES, William A. Radford. With a New Introduction by Daniel D. Reiff. Based on a rare 1925 catalog, this architectural showcase features floor plans, construction details, and photos of 26 homes, plus articles on entrances, porches, garages, and more. 250 illustrations, 21 color plates. 176pp. 8⅜ x 11. 0-486-47028-8

MY 66 YEARS IN THE BIG LEAGUES, Connie Mack. With a New Introduction by Rich Westcott. A Founding Father of modern baseball, Mack holds the record for most wins — and losses — by a major league manager. Enhanced by 70 photographs, his warmhearted autobiography is populated by many legends of the game. 288pp. 5⅜ x 8½. 0-486-47184-5

NARRATIVE OF THE LIFE OF FREDERICK DOUGLASS, Frederick Douglass. Douglass's graphic depictions of slavery, harrowing escape to freedom, and life as a newspaper editor, eloquent orator, and impassioned abolitionist. 96pp. 5³⁄₁₆ x 8¼. 0-486-28499-9

THE NIGHTLESS CITY: Geisha and Courtesan Life in Old Tokyo, J. E. de Becker. This unsurpassed study from 100 years ago ventured into Tokyo's red-light district to survey geisha and courtesan life and offer meticulous descriptions of training, dress, social hierarchy, and erotic practices. 49 black-and-white illustrations; 2 maps. 496pp. 5⅜ x 8½. 0-486-45563-7

THE ODYSSEY, Homer. Excellent prose translation of ancient epic recounts adventures of the homeward-bound Odysseus. Fantastic cast of gods, giants, cannibals, sirens, other supernatural creatures — true classic of Western literature. 256pp. 5³⁄₁₆ x 8¼. 0-486-40654-7

OEDIPUS REX, Sophocles. Landmark of Western drama concerns the catastrophe that ensues when King Oedipus discovers he has inadvertently killed his father and married his mother. Masterly construction, dramatic irony. Explanatory footnotes. 64pp. 5³⁄₁₆ x 8¼. 0-486-26877-2

ONCE UPON A TIME: The Way America Was, Eric Sloane. Nostalgic text and drawings brim with gentle philosophies and descriptions of how we used to live — self-sufficiently — on the land, in homes, and among the things built by hand. 44 line illustrations. 64pp. 8⅜ x 11. 0-486-44411-2

Browse over 9,000 books at www.doverpublications.com

ONE OF OURS, Willa Cather. The Pulitzer Prize–winning novel about a young Nebraskan looking for something to believe in. Alienated from his parents, rejected by his wife, he finds his destiny on the bloody battlefields of World War I. 352pp. 5³⁄₁₆ x 8¼. 0-486-45599-8

ORIGAMI YOU CAN USE: 27 Practical Projects, Rick Beech. Origami models can be more than decorative, and this unique volume shows how! The 27 practical projects include a CD case, frame, napkin ring, and dish. Easy instructions feature 400 two-color illustrations. 96pp. 8¼ x 11. 0-486-47057-1

OTHELLO, William Shakespeare. Towering tragedy tells the story of a Moorish general who earns the enmity of his ensign Iago when he passes him over for a promotion. Masterly portrait of an archvillain. Explanatory footnotes. 112pp. 5³⁄₁₆ x 8¼. 0-486-29097-2

PARADISE LOST, John Milton. Notes by John A. Himes. First published in 1667, *Paradise Lost* ranks among the greatest of English literature's epic poems. It's a sublime retelling of Adam and Eve's fall from grace and expulsion from Eden. Notes by John A. Himes. 480pp. 5³⁄₁₆ x 8¼. 0-486-44287-X

PASSING, Nella Larsen. Married to a successful physician and prominently ensconced in society, Irene Redfield leads a charmed existence — until a chance encounter with a childhood friend who has been "passing for white." 112pp. 5⅜ x 8½. 0-486-43713-2

PERSPECTIVE DRAWING FOR BEGINNERS, Len A. Doust. Doust carefully explains the roles of lines, boxes, and circles, and shows how visualizing shapes and forms can be used in accurate depictions of perspective. One of the most concise introductions available. 33 illustrations. 64pp. 5⅜ x 8½. 0-486-45149-6

PERSPECTIVE MADE EASY, Ernest R. Norling. Perspective is easy; yet, surprisingly few artists know the simple rules that make it so. Remedy that situation with this simple, step-by-step book, the first devoted entirely to the topic. 256 illustrations. 224pp. 5⅜ x 8½. 0-486-40473-0

THE PICTURE OF DORIAN GRAY, Oscar Wilde. Celebrated novel involves a handsome young Londoner who sinks into a life of depravity. His body retains perfect youth and vigor while his recent portrait reflects the ravages of his crime and sensuality. 176pp. 5³⁄₁₆ x 8¼. 0-486-27807-7

PRIDE AND PREJUDICE, Jane Austen. One of the most universally loved and admired English novels, an effervescent tale of rural romance transformed by Jane Austen's art into a witty, shrewdly observed satire of English country life. 272pp. 5³⁄₁₆ x 8¼. 0-486-28473-5

THE PRINCE, Niccolò Machiavelli. Classic, Renaissance-era guide to acquiring and maintaining political power. Today, nearly 500 years after it was written, this calculating prescription for autocratic rule continues to be much read and studied. 80pp. 5³⁄₁₆ x 8¼. 0-486-27274-5

QUICK SKETCHING, Carl Cheek. A perfect introduction to the technique of "quick sketching." Drawing upon an artist's immediate emotional responses, this is an extremely effective means of capturing the essential form and features of a subject. More than 100 black-and-white illustrations throughout. 48pp. 5 x 8¼. 0-486-46608-6

RANCH LIFE AND THE HUNTING TRAIL, Theodore Roosevelt. Illustrated by Frederic Remington. Beautifully illustrated by Remington, Roosevelt's celebration of the Old West recounts his adventures in the Dakota Badlands of the 1880s, from round-ups to Indian encounters to hunting bighorn sheep. 208pp. 6¼ x 9¼. 0-486-47340-6

THE RED BADGE OF COURAGE, Stephen Crane. Amid the nightmarish chaos of a Civil War battle, a young soldier discovers courage, humility, and, perhaps, wisdom. Uncanny re-creation of actual combat. Enduring landmark of American fiction. 112pp. 5³⁄₁₆ x 8¼.   0-486-26465-3

RELATIVITY SIMPLY EXPLAINED, Martin Gardner. One of the subject's clearest, most entertaining introductions offers lucid explanations of special and general theories of relativity, gravity, and spacetime, models of the universe, and more. 100 illustrations. 224pp. 5⅜ x 8½.   0-486-29315-7

REMBRANDT DRAWINGS: 116 Masterpieces in Original Color, Rembrandt van Rijn. This deluxe hardcover edition features drawings from throughout the Dutch master's prolific career. Informative captions accompany these beautifully reproduced landscapes, biblical vignettes, figure studies, animal sketches, and portraits. 128pp. 8⅜ x 11.   0-486-46149-1

THE ROAD NOT TAKEN AND OTHER POEMS, Robert Frost. A treasury of Frost's most expressive verse. In addition to the title poem: "An Old Man's Winter Night," "In the Home Stretch," "Meeting and Passing," "Putting in the Seed," many more. All complete and unabridged. 64pp. 5³⁄₁₆ x 8¼.   0-486-27550-7

ROMEO AND JULIET, William Shakespeare. Tragic tale of star-crossed lovers, feuding families and timeless passion contains some of Shakespeare's most beautiful and lyrical love poetry. Complete, unabridged text with explanatory footnotes. 96pp. 5³⁄₁₆ x 8¼.   0-486-27557-4

SANDITON AND THE WATSONS: Austen's Unfinished Novels, Jane Austen. Two tantalizing incomplete stories revisit Austen's customary milieu of courtship and venture into new territory, amid guests at a seaside resort. Both are worth reading for pleasure and study. 112pp. 5⅜ x 8½.   0-486-45793-1

THE SCARLET LETTER, Nathaniel Hawthorne. With stark power and emotional depth, Hawthorne's masterpiece explores sin, guilt, and redemption in a story of adultery in the early days of the Massachusetts Colony. 192pp. 5³⁄₁₆ x 8¼.

0-486-28048-9

THE SEASONS OF AMERICA PAST, Eric Sloane. Seventy-five illustrations depict cider mills and presses, sleds, pumps, stump-pulling equipment, plows, and other elements of America's rural heritage. A section of old recipes and household hints adds additional color. 160pp. 8⅜ x 11.   0-486-44220-9

SELECTED CANTERBURY TALES, Geoffrey Chaucer. Delightful collection includes the General Prologue plus three of the most popular tales: "The Knight's Tale," "The Miller's Prologue and Tale," and "The Wife of Bath's Prologue and Tale." In modern English. 144pp. 5³⁄₁₆ x 8¼.   0-486-28241-4

SELECTED POEMS, Emily Dickinson. Over 100 best-known, best-loved poems by one of America's foremost poets, reprinted from authoritative early editions. No comparable edition at this price. Index of first lines. 64pp. 5³⁄₁₆ x 8¼. 0-486-26466-1

SIDDHARTHA, Hermann Hesse. Classic novel that has inspired generations of seekers. Blending Eastern mysticism and psychoanalysis, Hesse presents a strikingly original view of man and culture and the arduous process of self-discovery, reconciliation, harmony, and peace. 112pp. 5³⁄₁₆ x 8¼.   0-486-40653-9

SKETCHING OUTDOORS, Leonard Richmond. This guide offers beginners step-by-step demonstrations of how to depict clouds, trees, buildings, and other outdoor sights. Explanations of a variety of techniques include shading and constructional drawing. 48pp. 11 x 8¼.   0-486-46922-0

Browse over 9,000 books at www.doverpublications.com

SMALL HOUSES OF THE FORTIES: With Illustrations and Floor Plans, Harold E. Group. 56 floor plans and elevations of houses that originally cost less than $15,000 to build. Recommended by financial institutions of the era, they range from Colonials to Cape Cods. 144pp. 8⅜ x 11. 0-486-45598-X

SOME CHINESE GHOSTS, Lafcadio Hearn. Rooted in ancient Chinese legends, these richly atmospheric supernatural tales are recounted by an expert in Oriental lore. Their originality, power, and literary charm will captivate readers of all ages. 96pp. 5⅜ x 8½. 0-486-46306-0

SONGS FOR THE OPEN ROAD: Poems of Travel and Adventure, Edited by The American Poetry & Literacy Project. More than 80 poems by 50 American and British masters celebrate real and metaphorical journeys. Poems by Whitman, Byron, Millay, Sandburg, Langston Hughes, Emily Dickinson, Robert Frost, Shelley, Tennyson, Yeats, many others. Note. 80pp. 5³⁄₁₆ x 8¼. 0-486-40646-6

SPOON RIVER ANTHOLOGY, Edgar Lee Masters. An American poetry classic, in which former citizens of a mythical midwestern town speak touchingly from the grave of the thwarted hopes and dreams of their lives. 144pp. 5³⁄₁₆ x 8¼.
0-486-27275-3

STAR LORE: Myths, Legends, and Facts, William Tyler Olcott. Captivating retellings of the origins and histories of ancient star groups include Pegasus, Ursa Major, Pleiades, signs of the zodiac, and other constellations. "Classic." — *Sky & Telescope.* 58 illustrations. 544pp. 5⅜ x 8½. 0-486-43581-4

THE STRANGE CASE OF DR. JEKYLL AND MR. HYDE, Robert Louis Stevenson. This intriguing novel, both fantasy thriller and moral allegory, depicts the struggle of two opposing personalities — one essentially good, the other evil — for the soul of one man. 64pp. 5³⁄₁₆ x 8¼. 0-486-26688-5

SURVIVAL HANDBOOK: The Official U.S. Army Guide, Department of the Army. This special edition of the Army field manual is geared toward civilians. An essential companion for campers and all lovers of the outdoors, it constitutes the most authoritative wilderness guide. 288pp. 5³⁄₁₆ x 8¼. 0-486-46184-X

A TALE OF TWO CITIES, Charles Dickens. Against the backdrop of the French Revolution, Dickens unfolds his masterpiece of drama, adventure, and romance about a man falsely accused of treason. Excitement and derring-do in the shadow of the guillotine. 304pp. 5³⁄₁₆ x 8¼. 0-486-40651-2

TEN PLAYS, Anton Chekhov. *The Sea Gull, Uncle Vanya, The Three Sisters, The Cherry Orchard,* and *Ivanov,* plus 5 one-act comedies: *The Anniversary, An Unwilling Martyr, The Wedding, The Bear,* and *The Proposal.* 336pp. 5³⁄₁₆ x 8¼. 0-486-46560-8

THE FLYING INN, G. K. Chesterton. Hilarious romp in which pub owner Humphrey Hump and friend take to the road in a donkey cart filled with rum and cheese, inveighing against Prohibition and other "oppressive forms of modernity." 320pp. 5⅜ x 8½. 0-486-41910-X

THIRTY YEARS THAT SHOOK PHYSICS: The Story of Quantum Theory, George Gamow. Lucid, accessible introduction to the influential theory of energy and matter features careful explanations of Dirac's anti-particles, Bohr's model of the atom, and much more. Numerous drawings. 1966 edition. 240pp. 5⅜ x 8½. 0-486-24895-X

TREASURE ISLAND, Robert Louis Stevenson. Classic adventure story of a perilous sea journey, a mutiny led by the infamous Long John Silver, and a lethal scramble for buried treasure — seen through the eyes of cabin boy Jim Hawkins. 160pp. 5³⁄₁₆ x 8¼.
0-486-27559-0

THE TRIAL, Franz Kafka. Translated by David Wyllie. From its gripping first sentence onward, this novel exemplifies the term "Kafkaesque." Its darkly humorous narrative recounts a bank clerk's entrapment in a bureaucratic maze, based on an undisclosed charge. 176pp. 5³⁄₁₆ x 8¼.   0-486-47061-X

THE TURN OF THE SCREW, Henry James. Gripping ghost story by great novelist depicts the sinister transformation of 2 innocent children into flagrant liars and hypocrites. An elegantly told tale of unspoken horror and psychological terror. 96pp. 5³⁄₁₆ x 8¼.   0-486-26684-2

UP FROM SLAVERY, Booker T. Washington. Washington (1856-1915) rose to become the most influential spokesman for African-Americans of his day. In this eloquently written book, he describes events in a remarkable life that began in bondage and culminated in worldwide recognition. 160pp. 5³⁄₁₆ x 8¼.   0-486-28738-6

VICTORIAN HOUSE DESIGNS IN AUTHENTIC FULL COLOR: 75 Plates from the "Scientific American – Architects and Builders Edition," 1885-1894, Edited by Blanche Cirker. Exquisitely detailed, exceptionally handsome designs for an enormous variety of attractive city dwellings, spacious suburban and country homes, charming "cottages" and other structures — all accompanied by perspective views and floor plans. 80pp. 9¼ x 12¼.   0-486-29438-2

VILLETTE, Charlotte Brontë. Acclaimed by Virginia Woolf as "Brontë's finest novel," this moving psychological study features a remarkably modern heroine who abandons her native England for a new life as a schoolteacher in Belgium. 480pp. 5³⁄₁₆ x 8¼.   0-486-45557-2

THE VOYAGE OUT, Virginia Woolf. A moving depiction of the thrills and confusion of youth, Woolf's acclaimed first novel traces a shipboard journey to South America for a captivating exploration of a woman's growing self-awareness. 288pp. 5³⁄₁₆ x 8¼.   0-486-45005-8

WALDEN; OR, LIFE IN THE WOODS, Henry David Thoreau. Accounts of Thoreau's daily life on the shores of Walden Pond outside Concord, Massachusetts, are interwoven with musings on the virtues of self-reliance and individual freedom, on society, government, and other topics. 224pp. 5³⁄₁₆ x 8¼.   0-486-28495-6

WILD PILGRIMAGE: A Novel in Woodcuts, Lynd Ward. Through startling engravings shaded in black and red, Ward wordlessly tells the story of a man trapped in an industrial world, struggling between the grim reality around him and the fantasies his imagination creates. 112pp. 6⅛ x 9¼.   0-486-46583-7

WILLY POGÁNY REDISCOVERED, Willy Pogany. Selected and Edited by Jeff A. Menges. More than 100 color and black-and-white Art Nouveau–style illustrations from fairy tales and adventure stories include scenes from Wagner's "Ring" cycle, *The Rime of the Ancient Mariner, Gulliver's Travels,* and *Faust.* 144pp. 8⅜ x 11.
                                                              0-486-47046-6

WOOLLY THOUGHTS: Unlock Your Creative Genius with Modular Knitting, Pat Ashforth and Steve Plummer. Here's the revolutionary way to knit — easy, fun, and foolproof! Beginners and experienced knitters need only master a single stitch to create their own designs with patchwork squares. More than 100 illustrations. 128pp. 6½ x 9¼.   0-486-46084-3

WUTHERING HEIGHTS, Emily Brontë. Somber tale of consuming passions and vengeance — played out amid the lonely English moors — recounts the turbulent and tempestuous love story of Cathy and Heathcliff. Poignant and compelling. 256pp. 5³⁄₁₆ x 8¼.   0-486-29256-8

Browse over 9,000 books at www.doverpublications.com

CPSIA information can be obtained
at www.ICGtesting.com
Printed in the USA
FSOW03n2027310816
24479FS

9 780486 420929